MILLIONAIRE INFLUENCER

50 STEPS TO YOUR ONLINE EMPIRE

YULI ZIV

ISBN 978-1544069388

For contact and other info visit www.YuliZiv.com

When you understand who and what you are, your radiance projects into the universal radiance and everything around you becomes creative and full of opportunity.
~Yogi Bhajan, Ph.D.

CONTENTS

Foreword by Aliza Licht...1

My Path to Influence...5

Introduction...9

PART 1:

SET YOURSELF FOR SUCCESS

1. Commit to One Year...17

2. Quit Your 9-5 Job..21

3. Define Your Purpose..24

4. Define Your Brand...26

5. Identify Your Unique Talents............................29

6. Be Aware of Your Weaknesses.........................32

7. Decide What to Keep Private............................35

8. Decide How Accessible You Will Be..................38

9. Experiment with Your Content..........................41

10. Become Obsessed with Consistency.................44

11. Don't Take Breaks Until You Get to the Top.....48

12. Choose What to Sacrifice.................................51

PART 2:

NETWORK YOUR WAY TO SUCCESS

13. Build Your Reputation...55
14. Make Millionaire Friends....................................58
15. Recruit Your Collaborators.................................61
16. Identify Opportunities Everywhere....................64
17. Stay on Top of Trends...67
18. Connect with Followers in Real Life...................70
19. Always be Broadcasting......................................73
20. Get Haters. Then Ignore Them...........................76
21. Project Positivity...79
22. Pretend as If You Already Made It......................82
23. Never Buy or Lie About Your Followers.............84
24. Get Rid of the Self-Promotion Guilt...................87
25. Be Grateful for Every Opportunity.....................90

PART 3:

GET YOUR BUSINESS IN ORDER

26. Establish Your Business Entity...........................95
27. Make It Easy to Find You....................................98
28. Define Your Audience..100
29. Make a List of Dream Clients............................103
30. Measure Yourself Against Your Goals..............106
31. Get Obsessed with Analytics.............................108
32. Work on Your Work Ethic..................................111

33. Always Over Deliver...116

34. Make Others Sell for You....................................119

35. Decide if a Manager or Agent is Right.............123

36. Manage Your Rates...127

37. Create Demand..131

38. Diversify Your Revenue Channels....................133

39. Automate Revenue Channels............................136

40. Create Tangible Products..................................140

41. Manage Your Cash Flow....................................143

42. Stay on Top of Money Collection......................146

PART 4:

MANAGE YOUR SUCCESS

43. Educate Yourself About the Industry................151

44. Study Your Clients...154

45. Get Basic Finance Knowledge...........................157

46. Get Basic Legal Knowledge...............................160

47. Learn to Negotiate..163

48. Learn to Say No...165

49. Learn to Hire...167

50. Learn to Lead..170

Acknowledgements..173

About the Author...175

FOREWORD BY
ALIZA LICHT

brand marketing & communications
executive, author of LEAVE YOUR MARK,
and former, DKNY PR GIRL.

~

The words "Fashion 2.0 Awards" scrolled down my Twitter timeline. It was 2010, and I was the anonymous social media personality, DKNY PR GIRL. It had been a year since I started tweeting as the elusive 'PR girl' and I wasn't about to blow my cover. But I love a good competition, and I wanted to win! Besides, DKNY PR GIRL was hugely popular. She was the first example of humanizing a fashion brand in social media, and this was going to be the first award ceremony of its kind for digital in our industry.

Founded by Style Coalition founder, Yuli Ziv, the Fashion 2.0 Awards were ambitious. I mean, who was this girl? She certainly wasn't a fashion industry regular. Yet here she was trailblazing new categories for us to excel in: Best Twitter, Best Facebook page,

Next Big Thing in Tech, Best Online Video, Best Fashion Blog, and Top Innovator. These were titles that the fashion industry had not contemplated prior to 2010 and had now become everything we wanted to be recognized for.

That year, DKNY PR GIRL was nominated for Best Twitter, and there was no way I wasn't going. I was behind that Twitter handle 24/7! We arrived at the venue and were asked to take some photos on the red carpet. Yuli was friendly and beautiful with a warm smile. I immediately took to her and she to me. It was exciting to see the event unfold and hear Yuli's vision for how digital would propel the fashion industry forward. I believed it and was eager to jump on the 2.0 train.

Yuli is a digital pioneer, and I believe that her true brilliance is seeing things others cannot. Way back in 2008, Yuli founded Style Coalition, one of the first blogger networks where she was both representing talent and putting brand deals together. She grew that business into a massive success, ultimately working with brands like Chanel, Dior, L'Oréal, Givenchy, Topshop, and many others. Yuli went on to write two books, and her book, *Blogging Your Way to the Front Row*, is still a best-seller!

Yuli has always been at the forefront of digital, experimenting and pushing boundaries. She is a connector of dots and a serial entrepreneur who has played a huge role in pushing the fashion industry into this new frontier, sometimes albeit, with brands kicking and screaming.

So what does Yuli know about influencers? Everything. As the person who launched the careers of some of the world's top bloggers, Yuli knows what it takes. She's the savvy business mind behind some of the world's most lucrative blogging deals and has not only cast talent for brands but has also created a proprietary software to measure the ROI (return on investment) on those deals.

Gone are the days where a pretty picture sufficed. We are also well past the idea that impressions or engagement matter in a vacuum. Breaking news, it's all about conversion. This is a real business and brands are spending serious money in this space. If you are a blogger or aspiring blogger who wants to have the talent deals like *Bryanboy* or *Man Repeller*, you better listen up. Your education starts right here with Yuli's impeccably mapped out strategy. It's a tough love, no nonsense crash course that will leave you motivated and inspired.

As the author of my own book, LEAVE YOUR MARK, I mentor a lot of young talent. Yuli is equally an incredible mentor in this book where she shares the step-by-step process of building your influencer empire. Yuli includes a healthy dose of advice, but also the insider trade secrets you can't learn from anyone else.

As a twenty-year fashion veteran in marketing and communications, I am the buyer of these deals. The strategy to create brand awareness has been revolutionized through influencers. You actually don't need to have millions of followers to build your online empire. Micro-influencers are changing up the game too with audiences who listen to their every recommendation. Creating that trust with your audience, being true to your brand, and having an authentic voice will help you navigate this ever-changing landscape.

That's the part you can control. The other part though is best left to Yuli.

The business of blogging is only getting bigger. The good news is that it's never too late to start. With the right advice and a stellar education, you can spend the rest of your days earning a pretty penny by doing what you love. Yuli will hold your hand along the way, and just when you think you've got this, trust me she will be ahead of you making sure you are prepared for whatever comes next!

Aliza Licht
New York
April 2017

MY PATH TO INFLUENCE

This year I will be celebrating fourteen years of living my American dream. I landed in New York City in July of 2003, just when the country was recovering from the 9/11 trauma and the internet bubble had burst. I sold all my modest possessions in Israel and found myself here with just one suitcase, a few thousand dollars of savings, and a work visa. It was a new starting point, and it was up to me to build myself up from there.

As uncertain as it sounds, I wasn't worried about starting over. After all, this wasn't the first time I immigrated to a new country. Back in 1991, right after the collapse of the Soviet Union, my family fled Russia and found a new home in Israel, thanks to my father's Jewish heritage. We also each brought just one suitcase and just one thousand dollars in our pocket. It was all we could get for selling our tiny one bedroom apartment in the working class "projects" of a typical southern Russian town, where being Jewish was a fact you try to hide. Landing in Israel felt like liberation.

Landing in America a decade later felt like finally finding home. I was accepted and given a chance to build myself up from scratch. I barely spoke any English and had even harder time understanding the hundred-miles-an-hour New Yorkers. But I knew I wanted to be one of them.

Eight years later, I was publishing my first book in English that went to sell thousands of copies and running a multi-million dollar company that was at the forefront of the digital revolution.

How did I get here? I never had a defined plan for success; I simply followed where my passion led me. In my early days in NYC, it was the heavy influence of *Sex & The City* that made me obsessed with getting into the fashion scene.

From the moment I saw the Bryant Park tents, where fashion week shows used to be, I wanted to get in. And my only way inside was starting a blog and becoming one of the first online fashion influencers. My live blogging from the fashion week shows often preceded the then slow traditional coverage and opened more doors than I imagined.

Then Twitter became a thing and allowed an outsider like myself to participate in online conversations with industry influencers like the DKNY PR Girl and others. I built my influence one tweet at a time, connecting with people who eventually helped me get where I am.

From my first blogger friends to eventual clients, my connections were mostly built online and through events I put together. Named Fashion 2.0, they became a symbol of the changing industry and eventually turned into big award shows recognizing digital fashion innovators.

I always said that I was lucky to be early in the space and carve out my territory. The truth is it took lots of hustle, sleepless nights, trials and errors to build the kind of influence that turned to be the foundation of my company – Style Coalition.

While I no longer influence people's opinions on fashion, I'm influencing the way this industry is marketing to its consumers. Through our network of some of the biggest lifestyle influencers, we've been able to launch new products, build up brands and inspire people.

Most importantly, we've helped hundreds of online influencers build their careers and turn their passion into flourishing businesses, empowering the new generation of business-savvy young women and men.

And that's a challenge that keeps me passionate today.

INTRODUCTION

Every year, millions of aspiring online content creators start a blog, a YouTube Channel, or an Instagram account. Only a few become multi-platform media moguls with a tremendous social influence that surpasses many celebrities, and some even join the so-called Millionaires Club.

It does represent the ultimate American Dream – self-made, talented, creative individuals who cultivate their audiences and eventually grow into recognizable brands and profitable independent businesses, often with a team of staff.

Influencer names like Chiara Ferragni now appear on *Forbes*' "30 Under 30 List," which states that she was on track to make eight million dollars in revenues in 2015. She started her blog, *The Blonde Salad*, in 2009, and by 2011 it was attracting a million unique visitors per month. Today, it is an online platform that includes a lifestyle magazine and an online store. With her own team of staff and multiple business franchises, Ferragni is a poster child of the influencer phenomenon.

So the question on the mind of every aspiring content creator is: how do I join that group of fortunate people who make a great living simply by being who they are and broadcasting their content?

It seems like many of these creators have the vision, the passion and the skills to succeed, but they never make more than just a supplementary small income.

What separates those who do succeed? Do they possess certain traits or follow certain rules? Perhaps it's a combination of both, but I truly believe in this day and age success as an online influencer can be built, if only you can commit to learning and constantly improving your skills. In this book, I've outlined the steps that would lead you to the top of your dream career.

While I don't have the secret formula to overnight success, over the past decade, I have witnessed firsthand the rise to stardom of many of the millionaire influencers and have noticed the patterns that make them successful.

I know from my experience that a six and even seven figure income is a reality for many of the self-made online influencers. As the CEO of Style Coalition, I personally signed six-figure checks for individuals, and through the years helped our influencers earn millions of dollars collectively.

I have witnessed their successes as well as their mistakes, and I'm here to help the emerging influencers make their way to building their businesses. In my opinion, professional skills and a business mind are necessary to sustain a long-term career in this new industry.

At Style Coalition, we have created influencer marketing campaigns for brands like Dior, L'Oreal, Bulgari, Guess, Sephora and more than a hundred others. By working closely with leading luxury and mass brands, I gained an intimate knowledge of what these brands are looking for in the influencers they choose to work with.

Who is this book for? Bloggers, Instagrammers, YouTubers, Snapchatters, and anyone who has started to build their online following and is now looking for motivation and practical advice on how to turn it into a serious business, support themselves financially, or build a bigger online empire.

The first two parts of the book are aimed to motivate and mentally prepare you for what it takes to be an online star, while the last two parts outline the business strategies that will lead you to success.

This isn't a beginners' guide. I covered most of the basics in my first book, "*Blogging Your Way to the Front Row,*" which I published back in 2011. Judging by the feedback I keep receiving from my readers, it is still relevant and has been called "the Bible for aspiring bloggers."

You can see the *Millionaire Influencer* as the next step, which many of my readers have been asking for. I'm excited to finally be able to share my most recent knowledge in this new, exciting, and growing space.

Let's dive right in!

MILLIONAIRE INFLUENCER

50 STEPS TO YOUR ONLINE EMPIRE

YULI ZIV

PART 1:
SET YOURSELF
FOR SUCCESS

1

COMMIT TO ONE YEAR

If you are reading this book, chances are you have tried creating content online. You've probably got your own online persona, some followers who occasionally share their positive feedback. You've seen some growth in traffic and followers and, on the surface, it seems like you are heading in the right direction in your pursuit of becoming an online influencer.

BUT. You probably also constantly feel like what you do is not enough and there are thousands of other online personalities trying to do exact same thing, with way more success. You feel like while your following base is constantly growing, it's not even close to the number needed today to be considered for those dream projects that only truly successful online influencers are working on. You've been doing it for a couple of years, mostly during your free time and weekends, and the results are very slow to show.

You start doubting whether you have what it takes to make it big, or wonder if there is a secret that others know and you haven't discovered yet.

I can guarantee you that people who succeed are not smarter or prettier than you, and they don't know all the secrets. However, they all have one thing in common. At some point, they decided to dedicate themselves to building their independent career online. They cut back on anything that took them away from their dream, and they decided to try and persist until they started seeing better results. They mastered their art, they sharpened their skills, and they listened to any feedback and advice until they started nailing it. THEY COMMITTED to making it work.

Can you commit to cutting back on some of your favorite activities, like TV, games or just wasting time browsing online, and instead learn new skills to improve as a content creator? Can you see yourself being completely consumed by your online persona and the content this persona broadcasts? Does that fulfill you and sound like a lifelong dream? Are you willing to sacrifice other priorities to give it a shot?

If the answer is yes, you must commit to one year of full devotion to this dream. Why one year? I believe one year is the ideal time frame; it is long enough to create change in yourself, learn new skills, and see results of your efforts. By creating this one-year goal, you put pressure on yourself to achieve it. You can also easily divide this big goal into monthly challenges, and see progress in smaller chunks of time. After one year, you should be able to have a clear picture of your growth trajectory, which should be exponential, ideally increasing every month by a higher percentage than the previous one. You should also be able to cross off several achievements from your dream list.

At the end of this fully committed year, you should honestly evaluate the results of your efforts against those goals and make a decision on how to proceed. If you indeed see the progress outlined above, the answer will be clear, and from that point, it will be only a matter of extending your commitment further and achieving greater results. However, if the success has been only partial or the progress had plateaued, you should have a tough conversation with yourself and either keep creating content as a hobby or move on with your life and look for other talents you can focus on.

I strongly believe one year is enough to discover whether you can make it in this industry. If you continue to pursue it as a profession without seeing significant results in your income or professional opportunities, eventually you will become frustrated and dissatisfied with your life.

You may argue that it took years for some of the current online influencers to get where they are now. It is true, but only because they started at a time when being an online influencer wasn't a profession, and the industry itself was just forming along with them. Now that the majority of consumer brands have established paid influencer programs as part of their marketing strategy, great content creators can earn revenue more easily through their craft.

Simply put, if by the end of one year of full commitment you were not able to secure even a small paid opportunity with a brand, this should be a red flag. If your blog traffic or social channels audience didn't consistently grow by at least ten percent per month during this year, your content doesn't strike a chord with your target audience. If your brand name didn't get noticed by the media, press, or your online peers, it probably didn't make a lasting impression.

It doesn't matter how much your friends and family are proud of you and your work – they are biased. You need the completely objective opinions of strangers in order to assess your work. If none of the recognition listed above has happened after one year – don't feel like a failure. There is nothing wrong with you, but you should probably not waste more time on this career. Find other pursuits that can uncover your true talent and earn you an income.

This advice is true for individuals and businesses in any area. If the universe does not reward you for your efforts, it means you should try a different path. However, if you are on the right path, the universe will keep sending you signs and encourage you to proceed. You just need to have a clear vision and be able to read these signs.

2

QUIT YOUR 9-5 JOB

Many people in pursuit of an online influencer career are trying to achieve it slowly while keeping their nine-to-five job. I can't blame anyone for their desire to have a steady income and a decent lifestyle. But here is the mistake: you can't have it all. You can only get to a certain point in your career as an online influencer without dedicating one hundred percent of your life to it and without being distracted by the duties and obligations of your daily job.

Of course, some jobs are more flexible and allow for some free time to think, plan, and test. Or you might be able to find a part-time job or freelance projects to keep you afloat. However, if they take more than 50% of your work day, most likely you won't be able to dedicate enough time, creativity, and brain power to your passion.

This holds especially true if you have a daily nine-to-five job that consumes most of your productive hours. First off, you won't have enough time in the day to compete with other creators who produce original content all day long.

Secondly, there is something about a daily job that squeezes out most of your brain and creativity.

Most people come home after a long day at work and need a break: a distraction, time with family and friends, and the list goes on. You must have tremendous discipline and an unbound passion to work on your own business while having a full-time job.

Most likely, you will be compromising on your performance in one of these two activities. If you invest all your energy in creating content and being an influencer and your employer takes notice, you may eventually lose your job. If you are giving your job one hundred percent of your energy daily (as you should when working for someone else), you won't be able to realize your full potential as an influencer.

Lastly, working full-time, you won't be able to accept all the networking, event, and travel opportunities that require a flexible schedule. A couple of years ago, we produced a campaign with an international brand that required a group of influencers to travel to Europe for a photo and video shoot. It was a lifetime opportunity for many. One of the influencers the brand had chosen to star in the campaign still had a full-time job and at that point was out of vacation days and couldn't get her boss to approve anything extra. We had to replace her at the last minute, which was unfortunate.

This is just one example out of many I've seen when a daily job gets in the way of fulfilling your dream. For some aspiring influencers, an opportunity like this would be the turning point to decide whether it's time to choose one path or another.

It is a big risk to quit your job, and you shouldn't be doing it unless you can support yourself for at least a year through savings, freelance projects, and are willing to cut your cost of living.

However, at a certain time of your life, you might have the privilege of being able to take that risk, especially if you don't have obligations like family, mortgage, student loans, etc. Ask yourself if not trying this would be something you would always regret.

If the answer is yes, and you are ready for sacrifice, failure, and all the consequences that come with it – you are ready!

3

DEFINE YOUR PURPOSE

Having a desire to succeed is simply not enough. You've got to have a plan!

First, you must ask yourself why you are doing it. What is the purpose of you creating content and sharing it with others? Are you looking to inspire others and bring more beauty into this world? Are you looking to educate people about the subject matter you are passionate about? Are you looking to connect with people who share similar passions?

You must have purpose in everything you do to create anything meaningful. Even a simple photo of your breakfast could have a purpose – it could promote healthy eating habits or help a local coffee shop to get the word out. Even the most trivial things in life have their purpose – don't underestimate it and don't be afraid to define yours as something small in scale or something very personal. You can make the world a better place even by taking small steps.

The bigger question you need to ask yourself is whether it's worthy of people's attention. In the internet age, content creators are constantly fighting for audience attention. If your purpose is completely self-ish, and you don't bring any value to your followers, your chances of success will be limited. The value you bring goes along with the purpose you defined. They must be aligned and work together, so your purpose must bring value to others.

Take mega-influencer Leandra Medine of *Man Repeller*. Her brand skyrocketed back in 2010 because she offered a fresh, humorous perspective on fashion. It's hard to believe, but fashion and comedy didn't mesh well until that point. Leandra, with her witty, often intellectual posts, showed that fashion could be funny and, most importantly, that you don't have to take it seriously. Seeing her rocking the most man-repelling trends with confidence broke the mold of what is considered feminine, sexy, and appropriate. It also inspired many girls to dress for themselves, and not for the men they are with.

Put some thought into your purpose before you start on this journey; otherwise, you may take a wrong path that eventually could leave you unfulfilled.

This is one of the reasons being an online influencer seems like a short-term career for many. To have longevity, it must fall somehow into a broader goal of your life and bring value to others.

Your online presence can evolve, but your purpose will always stay and be your compass.

4

DEFINE YOUR BRAND

When you decide to embark on this business journey, you must make one important switch. You must stop thinking about yourself as an individual, and start thinking like a business that has a defined brand, mission, value, rules, and goals. You must separate your private persona from the brand you are building online.

It may sound like the opposite of authenticity; however, the point is not to create a different persona, but to make a conscious decision about which attributes of your personality will become a part of your online brand and which parts will stay private, which parts may appear more dominant and which will need some polish to be appealing. Your online brand must represent certain parts of you in order to be authentic, but it doesn't have to represent all of them.

We all play different roles in our lives – mother or father, son or daughter, husband or wife, friend, manager. We have cultural and racial attributes that define us. Do they become part of your brand? There is no right and wrong; it's just a question of what do you feel comfortable emphasizing as part of your online persona and what would appeal to the audience you want to attract.

For example, your ethnic heritage can be a unique angle that makes your brand different from others in the same category and attracts an audience that identifies with you.

These decisions need to be made conscientiously because they will ultimately become part of your online brand and sometimes affect your ability to expand your business and attract certain clients.

Unfortunately, not all qualities that attract a large following also attract large clients. If your communication style is bold and direct, with occasional curses, it may gain you fans but can turn off big corporate advertisers who would prefer a safer choice as a brand ambassador.

The same goes for sexually provocative imagery – it certainly is a draw for online followers, but will most likely turn away brands that would be concerned about projecting that image. Most big corporations have several decision makers and sometimes even have their legal teams involved in choosing the brand's ambassadors, so projecting one extreme or another, unfortunately, may close some doors for you.

A classic and probably the biggest example is YouTube's most popular personality, Felix Kjellberg, known as *PewDiePie* who recently found himself in a scandal and lost some of his advertisers, as well as his partnership with YouTube after including anti-Semitic jokes in one of his videos. It took years for him to rise and amass his multi-million following and wealth. It took only one joke to damage his brand and start his downfall. In most cases, an apology would suffice, but it seems like in the case of *PewDiePie* it might not fix the damage.

It's hard to stay silent in the current polarizing political climate, no matter which side you support. There may be times you'll want to use your power as an influencer to change opinions and post on subject matters that are outside your usual scope. When you do so, you should proceed with caution and weigh all the pros and cons.

I have countless examples of brands that turned down our influencer recommendations only because they found one provocative photo in an influencer's Instagram or a post that expressed a bold opinion on a polarizing matter. Unless it's aligned with a brand's own stands, this would be a risk they might not be willing to take.

These choices make up your brand and dictate who you are going to attract as your audience AND your clients.

Having a defined brand will help you make difficult decisions like, for example, which opportunities to accept, how to react to critique, and determining the areas in which to expand your business. Of course, you can always adjust your brand image (or even change it completely), but it may cause you some frustration and even a loss of followers. Take the time to think before you act, and save yourself damage control later.

5

IDENTIFY YOUR UNIQUE TALENTS

As much as I'm advocating for being business savvy, having a plan, and defining your purpose, none of that matters if you don't possess any unique talents that you can share with the world. They don't have to be prize-worthy, but you must have some creative genes to be an online content creator. It could be writing, singing, styling, photography, or anything else that makes you unique.

Your talents are necessary especially in the beginning stages of your career, before you can hire professionals to supplement your skills. Early on, you will most likely rely on yourself to create your content, so first you must identify your strongest skills and continue developing them. We are lucky to live in the online age where information is easily accessible, so you can no longer use "I don't know how to do it" as an excuse.

If you decide that excellent photography is necessary for your online brand, you need to invest time and effort in studying and perfecting your skills.

These days, incredible equipment previously accessible only to pros has become affordable, so it's easier than ever to create beautiful content. In fact, professional-looking photos are a must when you compete in the marketplace with some amazing artists.

Kevin Burg and Jamie Beck, the duo behind *Ann Street Studio*, didn't stop at just incredible photography; they invented a whole new genre! Their cinemagraphs, still photographs with a minor and repeated movement, were first created in 2011 and since then became a major trend in commercial and editorial photography, turning Kevin and Jamie into some of the most recognizable names in the online influencer landscape.

While inventing a new photography genre is left to a select few, you should strive to create something unique. The only way to discover your talents is by constantly learning and pushing yourself to experiment. If beautiful photography isn't your natural skill, at the very least you can research mobile applications and filters that make your photos look more professional.

Many online influencers often post their tips and tricks, sometimes with a live demonstration of how they create the effects that make their content stand out. Many list the cameras and tools they use daily in the About or Resources pages on their blogs. A little bit of research on your favorite content creator can help find this information. Try to utilize some of these tools to create something new and original.

If all of that doesn't bring the results you are looking for, maybe video would be a better format to capture your content because you could focus more on your acting abilities or natural sense of humor.

YouTube is full of videos of the lowest quality that manage to bring millions of views, so looks are not the only way to get to the top. In your journey to discover your talents, you'll also have to find what works for your audience and continue developing those skills.

You can't be talented in everything, so it's a matter of what you decide to highlight. You have to be strategic with your choices, focusing on your unique talents and deemphasizing your weaknesses.

6

BE AWARE OF YOUR WEAKNESSES

As much as it's important to know your talents, it is also helpful to be aware of your weaknesses and stay away from exposing them. While as humans we all can have weak spots, as an online brand you must strive to look and sound professional. Since every piece of content becomes part of your brand, why would you want something you are not great at to be part of it?

If you don't sound great on camera, use a music soundtrack in your videos and keep the visuals as the focus. If your writing style is plain, say less and show more. It's rare to see someone who is a full package, but there are plenty of examples of content creators who have mastered just one thing and do it well.

The only exception would be if being bad at something is actually part of your content strategy. There is something humbling about it that followers love and can relate to, and it works for many. However, in those cases, exposing weaknesses was a conscious decision that is part of their online brand.

The worst thing that can happen is that your weakness will get exposed during one of your paid assignments, and in that case, you are risking losing a client over something that could have been minimized.

I learned this lesson the hard way with one of our top clients, who wanted to hire a well-known beauty YouTuber for a video campaign my company produced. The girl, who had millions of online followers, looked stunning in her own videos, which typically included how-to tutorials mastered by her while she listened to some pop tunes. In our video concept, we wanted to include a voiceover of the influencer, helping her audience to master the steps. Not once in the planning process did the influencer or her manager alert us that a voiceover wouldn't be her strongest suit or suggest that we should discuss alternatives.

When we came to a recording studio, we discovered not only that the girl couldn't properly read her lines and sound authentic, but her heavy accent would make it impossible for the viewers to understand her. Perhaps talking to the camera would have made it more understandable, but at that point, the production day was in full force and there was no time for any significant changes. The majority of the voiceover was not usable, which meant wasted production money on a recording studio, plus overages in post-production to solve the situation with subtitles.

Most importantly, one influencer's weakness became a challenge for our entire production team and was noticed by the client. All of that could have been avoided if the influencer or her manager alerted us about her weakness and gave us a chance to quietly resolve the issue prior to the day of the shoot.

Be upfront about the things you can and cannot do, and you will earn respect of your partners.

7

DECIDE WHAT
TO KEEP PRIVATE

Privacy is probably one of the things you will lose in some degree by becoming an online influencer. The nature of this business is to share deeply personal content that includes your appearance, your lifestyle, and your life events.

As time progresses, we are seeing more and more influencers sharing very intimate details of their daily lives – from giving birth to struggling with eating disorders and talking about periods. The audience often loves this openness, which brings them closer to their favorite online personality.

The good news is you are still in control of what you decide to share online, so if you feel uncomfortable sharing certain parts of your life – you don't have to do it. And while certain subjects are great traffic boosters, you don't have to go there to be successful. There are plenty of examples of online creators who separate their private life and family from their public persona and still keep their audience engaged.

You need to be comfortable with the content you are sharing, now and twenty years from now. Remember, even if you decide to delete something later, there is no guarantee people didn't download or take screenshots of that content. So make these decisions carefully.

I've seen plenty of influencers who became part of the industry for a few years and then chose to change their path. They may move on to become a lawyer, a TV host, or even a public service official. The content they created during their influencer career, especially if they used their real name, might be still accessible online, even if they deleted all sources.

This is one of the reasons many influencers choose to use a stage name that might be slightly different from their real one. When working with well-known personalities, I often learn the truth about their name only from their legal contract signature or a tax form. It would be smart for you to make that decision early, before your real name gets attached to any of your content.

Your personal content may also involve other people, such as family, friends or your children. Think of how sharing parts of their life will affect them and your relationship. Ask yourself if it's worth a few more "likes" from your followers. You may feel the pressure to be very open online after seeing how well it works for other influencers. However, there is something to be said about the enigmatic power of the information that is hidden. The mystery surrounding certain parts of your life may attract your followers and keep them on their toes with your updates.

Deciding what to keep private is as important for your brand, if not more, than what you post publicly. Don't fall into the trap of oversharing, unless it is part of your strategy.

8

DECIDE HOW ACCESSIBLE
YOU WILL BE

Whether you overshare or keep some things private, here is an important question to ask yourself: Are you creating a fantasy life most of your followers could only dream about, or broadcasting your reality, with its often not-so-pretty, rough moments?

The answer to this question will affect the accessibility level of your online brand. Are you a girl-next-door that every teenager in Middle America can relate to, or a privileged cosmopolitan jet setter that represents the one percent of the ultra-rich?

There is no right or wrong when it comes to accessibility. As long as you don't lose touch with yourself and, most importantly, reality, there will always be an audience that fits any type of content. Often the aspirational content that only a select few can afford drives large audiences who need an escape from their daily routine.

It is possible for you as a successful influencer to choose that route, even if you don't come from a privileged background, as at some point brands may start treating you to expensive clothes, free business class tickets to exotic locations, and other luxurious perks.

In the years I had the chance to be an influencer myself, I got treated to the most extravagant experiences. One night, a personal limo took me to a The Black-Eyed Peas concert, before which I was able to chat with Fergie, the lead singer, right before she got on stage. All that, courtesy of a major beauty brand she happened to be a spokesperson for. Another night, it was a one-on-one with Gwen Stefani on the day she was launching her new fragrance. How about a private breakfast for twenty behind closed doors at a famous New York City brunch spot with the one and only, Sarah Jessica Parker?

To top them all – there was a week-long trip to Morocco, courtesy of the country's tourism board. At one point, I found myself resting at the not-yet-opened Four Seasons Resort in Marrakesh in a room that would have cost me a thousand dollars per night. All this happened in the early days of influencer marketing, before brands truly knew the value of influencers. As you can imagine, these experiences would be multiplied today, especially if I had millions of followers.

The danger here is to ignore the value of the free perks you receive and forget the fact that most of your audience might not be able to afford the lifestyle you are promoting. You have to be conscious of the effect it will have on them – will they perceive it as aspirational and share your excitement, or will it create a gap that will be tough to conceal?

Whatever route you choose, always stay humble and grateful for the privileges you receive as an influencer.

9

EXPERIMENT WITH YOUR CONTENT

A great way to identify your strengths and weaknesses is to experiment with your content. Sometimes it's hard to predict what will resonate with people, as there is no precise formula for what works online. We've seen many blogs with gorgeous photography that barely get any readers, and, on the other hand, someone who posts very organic, unedited content that doesn't follow the rules of color and composition gets a high engagement.

Use the early days of your career as a content creator to test various approaches to see what resonates most with your audience. In order to do it right, you have to come up with a documented system to measure results, whether it's via Google Analytics on your blog or a simple count of likes and comments on your Instagram. Come up with a few categories of content and incorporate what's called an A/B testing, where you watch results for each category during a certain period of time and compare the metrics.

For example, during your travel coverage, compare photos of landscapes with photos of food or local culture. Or for a style influencer, photos of your look on a plain, minimalistic wall versus a city landscape. See what your followers respond to the most and eliminate the other category. Don't test more than two or three categories at a time so you can easily compare results and not confuse your readers. Add other categories slowly, and continue testing until you have a very clear idea of what performs best.

This doesn't mean you have to stick to one content category, but what you do include has to be a conscious and measured choice. After all, if your followers don't relate to your food photos, why would you continue feeding them? Food photography is a special skill, and doing it right requires some level of perfection. You don't have to master all genres of photography to be successful, so focus on your talents and content that speaks to other people.

The best plan is to create something that becomes your trademark look. It's that original spark that makes people identify your content immediately in the sea of others. It's a special moment every content creator should strive to achieve.

No one is more recognizable for their trademarked look than Susanna Lau, the British blogger behind *Style Bubble*. One of the inventors of personal style, Susanna's early posts from 2006 featured mostly coverage of designer collections and shopping trips. Luckily, Susanna's experimentation with her content and her personal style editorials led her to discover the trademark look, which took eclecticism to the next level. With her genius ability to layer, mix and match even the boldest patterns and colors, Lau inspired generations of personal style bloggers and became one of the most iconic and easily recognizable figures of the first generation of influencers. Over the years, she hasn't stopped experimenting within that lane, keeping her signature while staying fresh.

It is important, once you've found the general direction, to continue to polish and optimize your content, pushing creative boundaries and evolving. Creative experimentation always has to stay part of your content strategy to keep your followers surprised.

10

BECOME OBSESSED WITH CONSISTENCY

Consistency may sound like the opposite of experimentation, but it is absolutely necessary in order to maintain and grow your audience, as well as attract advertisers. Consistency touches all parts of your brand – from subjects to quality and volume of your content.

Once you've selected a category or a few on which to focus your content, steering away from it may hurt your brand. If you used to cover fashion, then suddenly decided that travel is your real passion, and now focus on beautiful sights more than your styling photos, you may lose some of your fashion followers. Most importantly, it may confuse potential advertisers who will have a hard time understanding your focus and identifying whether your audience is right for their brand. They need to be able to envision their brand alongside your content and feel comfortable with that.

The worst thing you can do is to decide to switch things up during collaboration with a brand. A couple of years ago, we worked with a well-known YouTube personality who was known for her fun and humorous beauty coverage, which resonated with many young girls. Our client, a huge retailer, chose her for those qualities and the ability to translate beauty trends to girls who are not necessarily obsessed with beauty. They signed the YouTuber for a long ambassador program, which was planned to run for several months. Somewhere in the middle of the program, she decided to change the focus of her channel completely, eliminating beauty from her coverage and therefore potentially losing that segment of the audience. Needless to say, our client was upset. Their sponsored content now appeared alongside funny videos that had nothing to do with beauty.

The only exception for when switching focus would be acceptable is life events that affect your persona and make it difficult to continue create content in a particular category. If your content focused on dating stories as a single and now you are married with a first baby on the way, it might be hard to stay authentic and continue these lines of stories, unless you decide to expand your team and hire other contributors or change the angle to readers' advice.

However, if you used to cover high fashion and then, after having a baby, decide to focus on the motherhood and its joys and challenges, you may have to strategize the transition. You may want to be open with your followers and talk about your lifestyle changes, bringing them along on your journey. You can have a slow, gradual transition or a clean-cut full-on rebranding. Whatever your strategy is, remember to think it through and communicate to your followers. Don't think they won't notice!

Another important consistency point is the quality of your content. Your followers consume your content because of its certain quality, and if that quality fluctuates, some of them may lose interest. Of course, if you purposely decide, as part of your content experimentation, to try different formats and styles – this could lead to great creative discoveries and become a positive thing. However, if the quality suffers because of your lack of time or resources – people will know it.

Most of the advertisers and brands that potentially want to collaborate with you will come to you because your content is well done. So if the quality is inconsistent, it may hurt their confidence in working with you because they won't be able to predict the quality of the final product and therefore the results.

Lastly, the most important thing that helps to steadily build an audience is your consistency in the timing and frequency of your posts. There is nothing that drives people more to the same online destination over and over than the reassuring fact that they will always find relevant, new content. Your readers have certain expectations when they visit your blog, Instagram, or YouTube, and no one likes to be disappointed if suddenly those expectations aren't met.

For example, if you say on your YouTube page that you post a new video every Friday, however you missed the last two Fridays, you may not get another chance from your subscribers, or they will simply visit less frequently. Be realistic with what you can commit to, and once you do, be disciplined with your schedule.

It is by far the most difficult part of being an online influencer – the constant pressure to create new content, even when you don't necessarily have the inspiration or time. It's easy to get lost for hours browsing Instagram or reading other blogs. It's easy to waste half the day perfecting a photo or a video. That's why discipline and scheduling are extremely important to your job as an influencer. You have to schedule your work day and stick to it, just as if you worked for someone else. Break down your typical week and then each day by hours, listing all tasks that need to be accomplished, including deadlines. Add all of these to your calendar and schedule reminders to keep you on track.

Once you start treating your hobby as a business, staying consistent and on schedule should become part of the job. As with any other job, you can't simply decide to skip work one day. You have a few annual passes for sick and personal days, but that's about it. You have to stick to deadlines, or you get fired. Apply the same rules to your online job, even though you are the boss and the employee.

11

DON'T TAKE BREAKS UNTIL YOU GET TO THE TOP

Discipline is one of those great qualities that are actually accessible to anyone, because it's completely trainable. Supposedly, the school system teaches us discipline, but I find that it's not always enough if discipline is not part of your nature. If you have been in a highly competitive, restricted environment such as a sports team, military training, or similar – you probably have the qualities needed to push yourself forward until you achieve the end goal. Everyone else has to work at it a little harder.

Without discipline and determination, I would have never finished this book. Finding time to write when running a business and juggling a family is not an easy task. In this case, I started writing it while pregnant with my first child, and continued through maternity leave and after coming back to work. That meant pushing myself to write on the weekends every minute when my baby was asleep. My ambition to release the book by a specified date kept me disciplined, even when all I wanted was to relax in front of the TV.

You will need these qualities if you'd like to do anything entrepreneurial in nature, including building your career path as an online influencer.

It is easy to get distracted with social activities, travel, and simply by your own laziness. Of course, we all need breaks to recharge, and you should dedicate some time to that.

However, taking longer breaks that will keep you away from your job can disrupt your growth and cause you to lose focus. It will also disrupt the consistency of your content and schedule. Your relationship with the audience needs to be strong so, when you do take a break, they'll stick around once you come back.

If you want to make it a reality, you have to dedicate one hundred percent of your time to your dream – at least for your first fully committed year. You will have more time to take breaks once your business is established and you have revenue streams that keep on producing even while you are on a break (more on that later).

First, you have to get to a point where you can afford to take a pause. Getting there takes lots of energy and determination. Don't discount that.

Most of the well-known influencers I've met on various projects are some of the hardest working people in the industry. It might look to an outsider as though all these people do is jet off to exotic destinations, eat, and pose. However, from what I've observed, professional influencers are always busy producing content. After all, this is the reason they get invited to experience all these amazing activities in the first place.

On every video or photo shoot we've done with influencers, as soon as the cameras stopped rolling, they were busy taking behind the scenes footage, editing it on the spot, posting, and communicating with their followers. It seemed like every minute of their day was dedicated to their career in one way or another. In every situation, be it business or pleasure, professional influencers think about their followers and whether it's something they would be interested in consuming.

The key is to enjoy what you do to the point that it doesn't feel work and becomes your life. In this situation, breaks are not needed because your experiences and the creative process constantly recharge you. This should be your goal as an influencer.

12

CHOOSE WHAT
TO SACRIFICE

On your way to the top, while you put one hundred percent of your time and effort into your new independent career, you will most likely need to sacrifice some other things in your life, or at least postpone them to a later date.

Sacrifice doesn't have to be a negative thing; it is simply reprioritizing your life so you can focus on your dream career.

Whether it's putting off your Master's degree or delaying to start a family or simply not taking that long trip to Europe to retain your savings – you have to prioritize your life accordingly and make changes that will allow you to dedicate your time without the feeling of missing out. This has to be your decision, something you are comfortable with and won't regret later on.

In this case, we are talking about just one year of full attention and focus to find out if this business is for you and whether you have what it takes to turn it into something profitable enough to sustain you. You can always reprioritize or come back to any of your bucket list items after one year if you don't gain enough traction. Or you can fulfill your other desires later on, once your business is established.

When it comes to sacrifice, it's important to establish timelines for revisiting your goals and priorities. If you decided to postpone having kids for a year or two, but find yourself caught up in your career and not able to stick to your original timeline, have an honest conversation with yourself if that's what you indeed want to do. Certain goals might be harder to achieve later on, so make sure you don't regret your choices.

If you make these decisions consciously and with purpose, these postponed things on your list won't hold you back from achieving what you want.

PART 2: NETWORK YOUR WAY TO SUCCESS

13

BUILD YOUR REPUTATION

As an influencer, you cannot operate in a vacuum. Whether you want to or not, you become part of the online community and part of the larger industry. People may rank you against your peers, compare you to others in your category, and try to guess your income level. They will also judge your personality, your communication skills, and work ethic. Whether you like it or not, your reputation in these areas will affect your potential work with advertisers and brands.

This is why building your reputation is crucial to your success. Every person you get in touch with will form their opinion about you, and you better be prepared and aware of the consequences. You never know where this person will end up in their career or how influential they may be to your success.

For example, some of your peers who started as influencers may end up taking a job in the PR industry after a few years. Or a brand representative who used to work on a small brand you didn't pay much attention to suddenly gets promoted, and is now in charge of a large advertising budget for a brand you've been dreaming of working with.

I have countless examples from my own career – one of my interns who turned into a client just a few years later, a friend of a friend who recommended me to a potential client, or a former boss who gave me my first big shot in my own business.

When you are a well-known online persona, people tend to talk about you. And in a small industry, if someone has a negative experience with you, it's almost guaranteed that the word will get out. It's a part of human nature; so don't give them reasons to share.

Being "blacklisted" by a brand because they had a bad experience working with you (or even if they just heard negative feedback from others) can ruin your entire career, no matter how talented you are. The problem with having a bad reputation is you probably won't know because most people won't tell you about it to your face.

The smallest thing can create a negative perception about you. From not meeting deadlines to being unwilling to incorporate feedback, people will form their opinions about you, and it will be hard to change them. Especially when it comes to in-person interaction. I've been on set with many influencers, and the majority always acted very respectfully toward our clients. However, there were also a few not so pretty examples of diva-like behavior and a lack of social skills when interacting with the client.

It is rare that an influencer asks about client representatives on set – their roles, titles, and level of decision-making. Considering that these are the people who give influencers their jobs, you have to get to know them and understand their roles in the process. This is what differentiates a professional who is a part of this industry from someone who is just there as a model or actor. The job of the influencer is to be both the creative and the business persona in order to navigate this space successfully.

Treat everyone with respect, and look at every person as if they are part of your growing career. Do not underestimate other people's influence on your own reputation, which is a big part of your brand as an influencer. After all, people want to work with those who are easy to deal with, always professional, responsive, consistent in their work ethic, and grateful for opportunities. Try to become one of those people.

It doesn't mean you have to say yes to everything and become overly accommodating. It's about being reasonable, polite, and leading with your business skill rather than emotion. This is a very important point to understand and work on. When you transition your persona into a business, you have to neutralize some of the emotions that will occasionally come up during your dealings with other people.

Why is it important? Because people who lead with their emotions are unpredictable and represent risk when it comes to business and a large advertising budget. No brand manager would want to risk their job by working with someone who is unpredictable.

If you treat yourself as a business and filter everything through a professional lens, rather than a personal or emotional one, you will build a reputation as a stable, pleasant person everyone loves to be associated with.

Your reputation is your gold, develop and nurture it.

14

MAKE MILLIONAIRE FRIENDS

Reputation is important, but how do you build it from zero when you are just starting out?

First, you need to build your network of peers who may help with advice, support, and hopefully open some doors. While making friends with other emerging influencers who are starting out just like you may be the easiest route, I suggest you make an effort to connect with influencers who are more experienced and accomplished than you are.

You need inspiration and motivation to succeed in this competitive business, and no one will teach you better than a peer who is already in the place where you'd like to be. Who knows, it may even bring them the satisfaction of helping out to someone who is in the place where they used to be just a few years ago. You must associate yourself with people who are where you want to be in order to lift yourself up.

Sound easier said than done? You are correct. However, if you develop a conscious goal to connect with someone aspirational and make efforts to achieve it, you have a better chance of getting there than someone who never tries.

You probably have a list of online personalities you look up to for inspiration. Have you ever reached out to one of them to try to make a connection? I know the chance they would actually respond is small, but there is one. If you reach out to twenty of your top icons with a proper message, I can guarantee at least one of them will respond.

What would be a proper message? You may compliment them on something specific they have done. Skip the generic "I love your work" stuff, and instead mention something special they have recently created and tell them what you liked about it. See if you can find something in common, like a hometown or mutual friends. Then continue with something actionable but simple. For example, a question about the software they used or a request to give feedback on your idea. Create a relationship by continuing the conversation every once in a while.

While email is still a great tool to connect with people who are typically hard to reach, meeting in person can be way more effective. These days, we have countless conferences and press events where influencers connect and network. Make a list of events and places that other well-known influencers attend often, and either buy a ticket or request an invite. (Yes, at the beginning you will have to ask for things and prove why you deserve them!)

Another possibility to connect could be a travel opportunity or a photo shoot project with one of your aspirational peers. At Style Coalition, we've done multiple photo and video shoots where emerging influencers worked alongside well-known stars, and it was great to see the friendships born out of these encounters. We always encourage our influencers to cross-promote each other's content and act as a support system for one another.

Use every moment together to create genuine connections with your peers and continue them online. For that to work, you have to project confidence, not try too hard, and avoid the stalker mode. If the other person is not interested in creating a connection – move on! This has to be a real and authentic relationship, built on mutual respect and willingness to help.

15

RECRUIT YOUR COLLABORATORS

Another crucial group of people you need to build connections with is potential collaborators – photographers, videographers, video editors, web developers, graphic designers, showroom coordinators, and everyone else who could contribute to your professional success. As they say, it takes a village... Build your own village of go-to resources who can help you out with any of your content aspects, either at the rates you can afford or as a trade for other services.

As your audience grows, it will be easier to barter or provide valuable promotion to your collaborators. As your revenues grow, you also will be able to budget for these services and afford highly talented professionals. However, at the beginning, you simply might not have the funds to do so, nor have the audience large enough to make it worthwhile to work with you for credit.

If paying for services is not an option, find individuals who are starting out just like you are and create mutually beneficial relations that help both of you grow. Don't be afraid to reach out to someone whose work you respect to try to create a connection. Don't lead with money or the lack of it. Take the time to get to know the person and figure out how your collaboration could benefit them. Ask them out for a coffee or a drink, and learn about their goals and challenges. Perhaps there is something you could help them out with as well. Most people love helping other people because it makes them feel good. You just need to be careful not to offend anyone with your requests.

This is where your network of peers will come in handy; referrals are the best way to find your collaborators. Ask if your influencer peers would be willing to recommend resources. The only problem you may encounter is competition. People may not be open to sharing their resources easily. Perhaps it would be a better idea to approach collaborators who work in a slightly different area or category than you. Another way to find resources is to research who other people are working with, without asking for a referral. Often you will be able to find credits within people's content and may try approaching individuals whose work you like.

Whatever you do – don't compromise on the quality of your content. If you are serious about your business, continue seeking resources that meet your standards and fit within your budget, no matter how small it may be. There are plenty of young and talented professionals who are in need of recognition just like you are. If you work on it diligently, you will be able to build a network of contacts that will help you outsource some of the content creator tasks and invest more time in strategy and creative ideas.

Here is where your skills as a creative leader and motivator are put to the test – can you inspire other people to work with you to help you get to the top? Can you make them believe in you and willing to help? Especially in the beginning, you will be relying a lot on the help of others to get to the top. Rallying talented people around you shows charisma.

16

IDENTIFY OPPORTUNITIES EVERYWHERE

Part of building your professional network is being able to identify opportunities and utilize them for your objectives. You have to invest your time and effort in connecting with people.

Typically, these opportunities to meet and connect with new people won't come your way organically. You have to seek them out and be proactive in pursuing them.

Let's say you spy an influencer or a photographer you admire sitting at the bar you just walked into. Would you have the guts to come by, introduce yourself, and make a memorable impression?

This is, of course, an extreme example that requires a certain type of outgoing personality, but it's also an ability that can be developed. After trying to talk to strangers a few times and getting a positive experience, you may realize it's not as difficult as you thought.

An easier route is connecting to helpful people via professional functions. Any type of events – from seminars to panels and conferences – is perfect because people in these kinds of places automatically turn on their networking mode. They are there to connect with others, just like you are.

It took me quite a few conferences and panels to feel comfortable talking to strangers. In the beginning, I would force myself to stay after a panel and talk to at least one of the speakers. I'd simply introduce myself, compliment them on their speech, and share a few of my own thoughts or ideas. It was easier than approaching a complete stranger because panelists usually expect people to talk to them afterward. In fact, from my own speaking experience, you want people's feedback right after to validate your performance.

The next stage of overcoming my fear was attending networking functions solo, without knowing anyone in the group. This way I wouldn't have a crutch – a person I know who I'd be tempted to talk to instead so I don't have to face strangers. There is something powerful about attending events on your own and taking the initiative to come up to someone, introduce yourself, and make small talk.

Most of my influencer connections were built during New York Fashion Week back in its early days. I would look for my peers in the crowd, or respond to their social updates from just a few seats away, and eventually connect in person. By following the event hashtag, I could easily see who else was in the room and even identify their location if they posted photos. Typically, if you've had several online exchanges, people will be very happy to meet you in real life. This is the way I've built my initial network, and it's been invaluable to me ever since.

As an influencer, you have to be able to network anywhere – at a party, brand event, conference, fashion show, or anywhere your potential audience may meet you. Get a stock of simple business cards with your brand name, social handles, and the easiest way to reach you, and carry it with you at all times. You never know where an opportunity may find you.

17

STAY ON TOP OF TRENDS

How do you discover these new online channels and build a significant audience on each with so much competition around you? The secret is to stay on top of social media trends and jump on board early, so you can capitalize on the audience that will be slowly discovering them later.

This is what's called being an "early adopter." Today, you have to be one of them in order to amass a significant audience on any platform. Often, these platforms will have a "recommended users" feature and encourage new users to follow their strongest content creators.

This is how Twitter gave a boost to its top users in various categories in its early days. When Pinterest launched, it was initially popular with many graphic designers and other creative types. When the masses discovered Pinterest, the early adopters saw their audience multiply day by day.

Textile designer Joanna Hawley, who has done work for Anthropology and Nordstrom, was one of them. In fact, she was one of the first Pinterest users and, as of 2017, boasts almost four million followers on the platform. Her Pinterest success led her to launch a blog under the same name, *Jojotastic*. When she launched the blog, she already had an engaged audience with whom she could share her posts. Obviously, in addition to being an early adopter, Joanna is a talented designer and content creator. But being on top of online trends helped boost her launch, and set her on a successful path as an online influencer.

It's hard to predict the future and know which social platforms will take off in a big way, especially when there are thousands of new apps launching every day. However, if you watch the space, certain signs can point to their future success.

For example, you may start noticing that other influencers cross-promote the new platform on their regular channels. This was the case with Snapchat, when suddenly many Instagrammers included their Snapchat name in their bio. When you see other early adopters embracing a network, you at least need to explore it and see if it's for you, so you don't miss out on the opportunity when it becomes popular. It's much harder to start building your audience after everyone is already using the platform and the tier of top users is clearly defined.

Another sign could be the buzz around a new platform within the tech circles or at events like South By Southwest, where many new social networks get their first spike of recognition. Back in 2007, a new app called Twitter was all the buzz at SXSW; in 2012, it was all about Pinterest and Instagram.

You can identify the next big social media network just by following the tech news and events. Websites like *Mashable* and *TechCrunch* are useful resources, and tech events like SXSW are a great place to network with the people who are building these platforms.

At the end of the day, as an online influencer, you are part of the social media and tech industry, and you have to stay on top of its trends to succeed. Develop your own sources of information that enable you to be in the know and, hopefully, take advantage of these new opportunities.

18

CONNECT WITH FOLLOWERS IN REAL LIFE

Building the personal bond with your audience that makes your relationship authentic isn't easy, especially since, as an online influencer, you are mostly communicating virtually. How do you connect with someone on a personal level and become their online friend if you've never met in real life? Building deep connections online is certainly possible, but nothing replaces an in-person interaction.

Make an effort to meet your followers in person whenever possible. This will establish a stronger bond and create loyalty, which is hard to achieve without a physical contact. By letting your fans see the real person behind your online persona, you will build advocacy among them.

You need that core audience of true fans who know you on a personal level, so you can rely on them when things get tough. Anyone who puts themselves out there eventually will run into negative comments, backlash, and even online bullying. These are the moments when you need your loyal followers the most – they can defend you when needed and help fight the negative reactions online. Especially if you've met in real life. After all, it's hard to post negative comments to a person you've met and connected with.

How do you meet your fans offline? There could be several opportunities that present themselves, and some of them you can plan.

Hosting events for brands seems to be the most effective way to invite your audience to meet you, and it provides an incentive for them to come. Whether it's a trunk show or a holiday sale, a new product launch or an advice session – it is flattering to be considered for a hosting gig, no matter how big or small the brand may be.

Especially in the beginning of your career as an influencer, don't underestimate an opportunity with a small retailer who is pursuing you, even if their budget is limited (or non-existent). Think about it as a party someone is willing to throw on your behalf, and feature you as the star of the show. It positions you highly with your audience, and most importantly, gives your fans a chance to connect with you in person.

If these types of invitations are not coming your way, be proactive and approach a local store or even a bigger retailer. Sometimes you will be surprised by how often they may be responsive to your idea of hosting an event with your followers. After all, their cost may be only a few bottles of sparkling wine and longer open hours. However, if you do approach a brand proactively, you need to make sure you can actually deliver and bring at least a small number of potential customers to their store.

You can start small and get to practice your hosting duties, get a better estimate of how many people will actually show up, whether they shop, and what value you can bring to a brand. After getting a few events under your belt, you can establish your hosting rate and turn it into a profitable revenue channel.

Approach these events strategically – it's not always about how much money you can make. Some career moves are more about the bigger picture: your brand and positioning as an expert and authority.

As you become more recognizable to your audience, events may not be the only avenue to meet your fans – you may be meeting them on the street, in restaurants, and airports. Always take the time to connect, even if only for a brief moment. Cherish these connections, because they build your core fan base. Give them a shout out, take a photo together, compliment them, and be grateful for their attention. Most importantly, do all of this genuinely.

No matter how introverted you are in real life, you have to make an effort to connect with people. Believe it or not, some of the most seemingly outgoing influencers I've met throughout my career turned out to be extreme introverts in real life. They managed to turn on their personality on Snapchat and YouTube, but when it came to social interactions, they were completely closed off. However, once a fan approached them, they always lit up and gave their best effort to appear humble and gracious for the attention.

Social skills, if they don't come to you naturally, need to be acquired if you wish to become successful in this business of influence.

19

ALWAYS BE
BROADCASTING

Once you start building your platform and see it slowly grow, it is important to keep the connection with your audience going. In our fast-paced digital world, if you stop broadcasting for just a few weeks, or even *days*, you may be forgotten. Your content strategy has to be consistent, diverse, and most importantly, frequent.

Luckily, these days you have a variety of channels that are built for short-form content, so broadcasting and publishing doesn't take as much effort as it used to do.

Before the rise of Twitter, Instagram, and Snapchat, influencers had to rely on blog posts or YouTube videos to connect with their readers, and many spent hours crafting a meaningful message, shooting, and editing pictures or video before they could post it.

These days, beyond the short-form content channels like Twitter and Instagram, we also see the Snapchat phenomenon that encourages real-time, unedited broadcasting of snippets of your life, and it doesn't require extra time to edit and perfect the message. In fact, the more raw, real, and authentic the content looks, the higher engagement it gets.

You may think this contradicts the advice for producing quality content, but you should not be replacing your beautifully edited blog post photos or Instagram pictures with stories and snaps. You should be supplementing it instead, using various short-form channels to broadcast and connect with your audiences as frequently as you can.

For example, you may publish a new blog post twice a week, add a new YouTube video once a week, post an Instagram photo daily, ask your Facebook followers to chime in on your latest content several times a week, and have an ongoing behind the scenes Snapchat story developing daily.

If you strategically plan every story across multiple channels, you don't need to come up with different concepts for each; they could highlight various aspects of the same story – some more edited, some raw and spontaneous.

This strategy creates dimension and adds to your value as a content creator. Which in turn makes you more attractive not only to your audience who likes to experience your different sides, but also brands that could potentially see themselves as part of your multi-channel coverage. Some brands may want to tap into your YouTube skills, and some could utilize your Snapchat. By broadcasting on multiple channels, you expose yourself to different opportunities. By doing it often, you sharpen your skills and increase your overall engagement.

How do you stay always on? Until it becomes an organic part of your life, the answer is proper planning. Look at your calendar for the week, and identify which events and occasions could be appropriate to broadcast on which channels. Or take each event and think what types of content could be created there. Perhaps you can produce multi-channel coverage, resulting in different outtakes. If it helps, create calendar reminders for your Instagram stories.

Think in advance about the type of shots or messages you'd like to broadcast from that event or occasion. This way, you will be focused on getting the coverage you planned and able to enjoy what's actually happening. Many of the spontaneous moments you see online are carefully planned editorials, created with the influencer's brand in mind. Just like reality TV is full of planned "spontaneous" happenings, your coverage should have a mix of authentic moments that still fit within your online brand. And just like TV always has something interesting to consume on every channel you flip through, your influencer persona should constantly be broadcasting and supplying viewers with original content.

20

GET HATERS, THEN IGNORE THEM

The biggest challenge of putting yourself out there online and experimenting with your content is the criticism that comes with it. As an online influencer, you must be able to deal with differing reactions and even sometimes manage your personal brand crisis.

Let's differentiate between two kinds of critics. The first are those who disagree with your statements and opinions by providing valid arguments or backing up their critique with some knowledge in the area. They may point out certain issues in your content, or argue with your point of view, skills, expertise, talent, etc. Even in matters of taste, they express their opinion politely, without hurting anyone's personal feelings. You can defend yourself and use it as constructive criticism to get better at your craft. However, you should avoid the danger of adjusting your content just to cater to people's opinions and tastes.

If your brand is strongly defined and you know your values, this should not happen. It's when you start listening to the critics and doubting yourself that you run into danger.

You also have to weigh all feedback proportionally – what percentage of your audience often criticizes your work? Sometimes we have the tendency to focus on one or two negative comments in the sea of positive reactions, and let that small group affect our mood, our motivation, even our purpose. Avoid this trap!

The second group of haters is simply negative for the sake of it and more difficult to deal with, as the reasons for their hate are not always rational – it may be jealousy, their own issues projected on you, or even their own mental struggles. No happy person ever goes online just to spread hate, so have empathy for these people who struggle to find themselves. Most importantly try to ignore them, so they don't affect your craft.

At some point in your career, haters will become an inevitable part of your audience, and in some ways, they could even be seen as part of your success. After all, they wouldn't care about you if you were an obscure person. Haters need an audience, and they came to you because you have built one.

I know ignoring them is easier said than done, but this is one of the biggest tests to find out if you are cut out for this career. Are you able to detach yourself as a private person from your online personality, and not take into heart people's opinions about your online self? Can you stay strong and unaffected by these often-hurtful attacks?

Observe your reactions and ask yourself: Why do I react a certain way to certain comments? Does it push a button? If so – try to identify your reasons for taking something so personally and getting hurt by strangers that don't even know the real you.

The best way to withstand the negativity directed toward you is by building your spiritual strength, whether it is through meditation, religious practice, self-development books, or other methods. This should become a part of your everyday life so you can handle the ups and downs that come with online fame and exposure. Your stamina needs to be developed, just like a muscle.

Another important thing that may help to you along the way is building a trusted personal circle of friends and family who know the real you and can always remind you who you are. The foundation of your everyday reality and the people in your life can keep you grounded and unaffected by the sometimes-harsh reality online.

21

PROJECT POSITIVITY

As an online persona who influences people's opinions, you have the responsibility for the content you produce and the online messages you put out there. Think carefully about what you project and how it affects your followers. This is especially important if your follower base is on the younger side and looks up to you as a role model.

From your body image to your opinions about world events, and the ways you handle criticism – you are being watched and listened to every time you post online. Use this power wisely.

When it comes to controversial subjects, the general suggestion would be to keep things neutral and positive, especially if your typical content falls within the lifestyle area and is simply meant to be inspirational and creative.

However, sometimes it is hard to stay neutral in a world where political disasters happen daily, and people are being attacked on the basis of race, religion, or simply their way of living. You should be using your platform to project patience, tolerance, and diversity.

However, if your views are bold and somewhat controversial, you have to consider the potential consequences on your career carefully. You have to accept the fact that some of your audience may feel alienated and even stop following you all together.

When it comes to hot topics, try to look at each situation from the lens of your personal brand and business. See if the issue fits into your mission. If it doesn't, maybe it shouldn't be expressed on your branded, public channels. A solution to that may be keeping a separate profile for your private persona, where you can express yourself without filters. Or even keeping that profile private and accessible only to friends and family.

Just like with controversial social and political issues, the same rules apply to your personal frustrations and venting. Let's face it, all of us have been in situations when online venting and complaints seemed like the only way to feel better – from airport security to bad weather and simply things that go wrong.

Everyone needs to vent once in a while, however it's easy to fall into the temptation of sharing these types of reactions with your followers. After all, it is comforting to have the instant support of the people online. You can certainly use your follower base for comfort in some instances, but be careful not to turn into a constant complainer.

Your potential clients will be reading your posts and may get concerned about your complaining nature. No one likes to see their content mixed in with someone's set of frustrations.

If you do decide to express your bold opinions or personal issues publicly, focus on communicating the positive message. Try to find it in every scenario. Every difficult situation teaches us a lesson, and every world disaster brings people closer. Remember that, and focus on the community you have built – what are they looking to get from you? Support, a positive example, inspiration? Be their lighthouse.

22

PRETEND AS IF YOU ALREADY MADE IT

Pretending to be anything you are not may sound like bad advice, but in this case, we are talking about your confidence. When it comes to online influence, confidence affects your brand and the way your audience sees you. After all, how can you inspire people if you are not comfortable in your own skin? As someone who constantly puts yourself out there, you must project a confident, successful image. Most importantly, you have to believe in it. Often your perception of yourself is what's holding you back from achieving the next level of success.

My favorite yoga teacher used to say anytime a pose would be too challenging or seemed impossible to achieve: "Fake it till you make it!" meaning by faking the result as much as you can, you actually practice and eventually attain it.

Practicing your confidence is just like practicing a yoga pose. Sometimes it needs faking until it comes naturally. If you pretend to be confident for some time, eventually it will become part of who you are. You constantly have to lift yourself up to grow. In this case, you have to focus on the prize – your goals and dreams – versus today's reality. It's about imagining where you want to be and practicing that visualization daily, so it becomes part of your reality down the road.

If you get caught up in the current stage, constantly analyzing and worrying about what you are missing, you will never grow. In this fast-paced space of online influence, it's all about growth – of your audience, your brand, and your business. You always have to think a few steps ahead and stretch your goals. This is where pretending or faking it in your mind helps you achieve real growth. By convincing yourself that you are on your path to success, you create that reality and you live it. Your mind makes space for the opportunities to come and for success to grow.

The obvious danger is that sometimes the success is never achieved in reality, and you are left with a fake perception of yourself. So you have to be aware of this technique and not take it too far. The pretending aspect is more of a visualization of yourself that gets reflected in your online content – your very own aspirational persona.

Create the person you dream to be through your online content, and you will slowly become that person. See yourself as a successful entrepreneur building a long-lasting brand and start acting like one, shaping your reality.

23

NEVER BUY OR LIE ABOUT YOUR FOLLOWERS

While on the subject of pretending, we have to address another sensitive issue that exists in the online influencer community. It has to do with buying followers in order to fake the size of your audience, and therefore, influence.

Unfortunately, doing so today couldn't be easier – there are many tools that automate the process effortlessly, and the price is lower than ever. As much as the social platforms attempt to clean up the system once in a while and catch online bots that create fake followers, they can't catch them all.

It used to be easy to spot someone with a fake following because they would have a significant amount of followers but no real engagement with their content. For example, less than 1% of their audience would ever "like" or comment on the content. This is always a red flag. It points to a lack of engagement, regardless of whether followers are fake or real. However, once people started watching for engagement rates, a new generation of bots came to market, and now they fake likes and comments as well. Buying content "likes" couldn't be easier these days, which unfortunately makes it a tempting practice for many. You start thinking that everyone is doing it, and you have to keep up with your peers at any cost.

For me, as someone who helps influencers monetize their audience, there is nothing more frustrating than discovering fraud and realizing the influencer you are trying to convince your hard-earned client to work with is not what they claim to be. This is a huge issue that undermines everything we've ever built and fought for. It took me years to convince my first client to invest in influencer marketing. We've come a long way since then, but all it takes is one bad apple to spoil the bunch. And in this regard, it's more like *several* bad apples. Coming across a case like this often drives brands never to work with influencers on a larger scale and invest their marketing money elsewhere.

Luckily, various tools have been built to discover fake followers and call out the influencers who buy them. Brands are looking for active audience participation and comments that engage in a real conversation. If a post falls on deaf ears, it often raises a red flag about the legitimacy of the influencer's following. If you dig deeper and look at the profiles of people who liked the content to make sure they are real, as well as read the comments and look for meaningful responses, you can still tell the difference between someone with a genuine audience and someone who is a fraud that relies on bots to create engagement.

Besides the fraud aspect, why is this practice dangerous? First, once you are suspected of buying your following, your reputation is damaged. Second, if brands measure the impact of a campaign on their end and find that your content didn't create any effect – they will never work with you again.

Lying about your audience is always a short-sighted practice that eventually gets exposed. If your goal is a growing career path in this industry, honesty and integrity have to become part of your brand.

24

GET RID OF THE SELF-PROMOTION GUILT

Most successful entrepreneurs share a common thread: they are good at self-promotion. Not the shameless type that alienates people, but the kind that simply acknowledges their achievements and successes, and shares these moments with others.

Self-promotion guilt is another obstacle you might discover on your way to the top, and it might be there for multiple reasons. Generally, bragging is considered to be an inappropriate behavior by society. When it comes to women who brag, the perception is even worse – many cultures still encourage women to be demure.

However, as an online influencer, you are in the business of marketing and must market yourself and your brand, celebrate milestones, and announce achievements.

You have to start thinking of yourself as a brand and a company, so there is no room for self-promotion guilt. In fact, companies spend a big chunk of their profits on marketing and see it as a positive investment in growth. So you, as a business, have to invest in your own PR and marketing as well.

How do you do that? When you achieve a certain number of followers or get invited to a show by your favorite artist or get to work with your idols – talk about it. Highlight why it is significant to you and how this achievement impacts you and your business. Don't be afraid to talk about the difficulties on the way. Ideally, your achievement will inspire others. In this instance, it wouldn't be perceived as a self-promotion.

The key in every bragging act is to remember how you got there and who got you there. In your case as an online influencer, it is most likely due to the size of your audience, so don't forget to express your gratitude to them.

If you are part of a group of influencers participating in something worthy of bragging – don't forget to acknowledge them. Success tastes better when shared.

Most importantly, stay humble. When you show humility, it is hard for people to blame you for being self-promotional. So practice these qualities and work on sharing your successes.

Unfortunately, I've seen countless cringe-worthy self-promotion acts by online influencers. I remember getting a press release in an email, announcing influencer X achieving a million-readers milestone. While I can't argue the validity of the number itself, the tone of the press release was taken from a global corporation announcement, with quite a few exaggerations.

This is the type of self-promotion that has an opposite effect on people: instead of inspiring others with your success, it raises eyebrows.

Be careful not to inspire disbelief or jealousy with your self-promotional tactics. Think about the value you bring to the reader. As an influencer, that's your responsibility.

25

BE GRATEFUL FOR EVERY OPPORTUNITY

We've talked about being grateful in almost every chapter of this book, but it is such an important aspect of your success that it deserves its own mention and more detail on how to put it into action.

You always have to remember that being an online influencer is a privilege – it's a creative, independent career that many people dream of and only a select few manage to make a reality. As an influencer, you are often invited to various events, treated to all expenses paid trips to exotic destinations, gifted expensive products, and offered large sums of money for doing work you enjoy.

Remember: all of these opportunities are given to you by someone who noticed your craft, skills, passion and dedication among many others like yourself. That person who wrote a "yes" next to your name on the list or gave approval on the budget to hire you – they deserve a thank you. And you will be surprised by how rarely these people get to hear that.

As someone who has given once-in-a-lifetime opportunities to hundreds of influencers and paid out millions of dollars' worth of compensation for influencer campaigns, I can tell you that even a simple "thank you" is a rare thing these days (not to mention a more elaborate version in the form of a physical thank-you card). Occasionally, I would get a Christmas card thanking me for the work we've done together, but as the industry has been growing and opportunities multiply, these cards come in less often. The appreciation for something that was so hard to achieve just a few years ago is now pretty much gone.

I realize giving these opportunities is part of the job I've chosen, and I don't expect a thank you for every single one of them. However, those who did take the time to express their gratitude will always be remembered. This is especially true with the people you work with on a daily basis – brand marketers, project managers, producers. I feel particularly thankful when my team gets treated to a box of cupcakes or chocolates by one of the influencers they just worked with. It makes them feel appreciated and motivates them to be best at what they do. A small show of appreciation from a partner goes a long way!

Use your gratitude as another opportunity to connect with the people who have enabled your career, and make sure to leave a positive memory. Remember that no one owes you anything and that the only reason people work with you or for you is that they have chosen to do so. They have chosen to spend their time and efforts on helping you out, and that is a huge commitment.

I will never forget how, a few years ago, one of the influencers who recently joined our network asked to have lunch with me and threw a surprising question at me even before my food arrived: "What have you done for me so far?" I was stunned. I didn't expect such direct confrontation. Granted I hadn't brought her a million dollar deal yet, but I also had no obligation to do so. Over the next few years we worked quite a lot together and some of the opportunities my company provided to that influencer significantly raised her profile, but I couldn't forget that lunch, even several thank-you cards later. To me, it epitomized the lack of appreciation that is so common these days in our business.

The opportunistic attitude is so short sighted and focuses only on the immediate gains, which is a mistake many influencers make. Because the industry is so young, they don't see longevity as a possibility at all. There aren't enough examples of online influencers lasting for over a decade and building successful businesses. Hopefully, this will change soon, and people will realize this is a long career that you are building step by step and the way you position yourself in the early stages is very important.

Make gratitude part of your every step.

PART 3: GET YOUR BUSINESS IN ORDER

26

ESTABLISH YOUR BUSINESS ENTITY

Now that you've got yourself and your online brand in order, you need to organize your business properly.

If you are truly serious about your craft, you have to consider establishing your business entity early on. It will help separate your business from your personal affairs, and your income as an influencer from any other income. It will allow you to view and manage your finances clearly and will make your clients take you more seriously. Large companies and brands always prefer to work with business entities rather than individual contractors.

When is the right time to establish a legal business entity? For my company and me, it was when I sold my first large campaign to a potential advertiser. I had to invoice for a five-figure amount and needed a legal business name to be accepted as a vendor. Once I had the company established, it gave me the confidence to start treating my idea as a company.

It may not make sense for you to establish a business without having any significant income, because you can continue reporting it as a personal income. However, the price for creating an LLC (Limited Liability Company) is so small these days and can be done online in just a few clicks. Yes, you have to consider some extra work on your tax returns at the year's end, so the total annual income has to be worth that extra step and the additional expense. Your best bet would be to get advice from an accountant familiar with small businesses and explore all options and costs.

Once you have an entity, you can start expensing certain things related to the business you are building, so the extra costs of establishing an entity may be recouped within a year.

Another great thing about having a business entity is that you can hire people. I know it sounds like a stretch in the beginning, but you may need the help of other freelancers or eventually have your very own assistant. In order to pay them, you should also establish a business bank account and make sure all business income and expenses get routed through it. It will allow you to easily track business income and expenses and create a discipline of separating personal finances from your online business.

For the advanced students among you, who truly want to be in charge of their finances and business growth, I would highly recommend getting an online accounting software subscription and connecting your bank account and business credit cards to it, so you can easily watch expenses, categorize them and generate reports in one click. At some point, when you hire a bookkeeper it will be easy to give them access and share all of your accounting history. Knowing how to access your financial reports puts you in control of your business, reducing the need to rely on other professionals, which is a huge advantage while you grow.

It will make your tax preparation at the end of the year a piece of cake and will give you better visibility into your progress throughout the year. You also will be able to track all client invoices and easily send reminders. For a small monthly subscription, you can be your own Chief Financial Officer with very little help.

I learned QuickBooks entirely on my own and was managing business finances without a bookkeeper for the first couple of years of my business. Obviously, as you grow, you may need one for a certain number of hours per month, which is again a business expense.

Most importantly, when you have a business entity, you behave like a business and have the responsibility to grow it. Take the leap of faith and start not only treating yourself as a business, but being one.

27

MAKE IT EASY TO FIND YOU

Now that you are a business, think about how you will be marketing your services and attracting clients. Of course, in the beginning, you might have to be proactive to land your first few clients.

You may reach out to a few potential targets – brands you would like to work with – and tell them about yourself. But the smart way is to put all the information on your website and make it easy for potential clients to find you. This includes an easy way to contact you, which should be your email, not via Direct Message on Instagram or Snapchat!

You will be surprised to know how many blogs still use the generic contact form as the only way to get in touch. Every time I use one of these forms, it feels like the message is being sent somewhere to the universe and you can only hope a human would actually read it. If publicly posting your direct email address overwhelms your inbox, create several email aliases for your domain, to serve different purposes. For example, one could be given to your readers, another one to potential clients, and a different one to editorial and press contacts. Even if they all come into the same inbox, you can separate them into folders and make it easier to manage. This way you can create a special filter for your advertising inquiries and make sure you don't miss anything urgent.

Another important piece of information to include is your bio, and your age if you are comfortable sharing it. Knowing these details helps potential advertisers tremendously. Some products have strict age restrictions. For example, if you look younger than you are, potential clients may overlook you for that opportunity.

Another important piece of information is your location or residence. If you share your time between two cities, note that. Your location could be crucial in booking you for a certain project. Some brands may not have a travel budget and prefer to work with local influencers. Or the opportunity might come up at the last minute, and it would be good to know if you could be locally available.

Make this basic info easy to find on all of your social channels, not just your website or blog, to increase your chances of being contacted for specific opportunities. Don't assume people have time to do a background check and spend time browsing all your profiles to find this information. Make it easy for them to find you!

28

DEFINE YOUR AUDIENCE

Another effective way to help your potential clients to select you for various paid opportunities is to help them identify your audience. Many marketers will foremost look at your audience to understand if you are right for their brand.

For example, if most of your followers are young students or professionals at the beginning of their career who can't afford luxury products, you may not be right for these types of brands.

One exception would be luxury beauty products, which often become aspirational and still accessible for a younger audience with limited resources. While they can't afford Dior shoes, they can purchase Dior lipstick as a treat for a special occasion. That's why many luxury beauty brands do target a younger audience – they want to create an aspirational tier of consumers who may purchase a lipstick today and an expensive shoe from the brand years later, once they have a stable income.

Income level is not the only important metric when it comes to your audience. Their gender, marital status, kids, location, and education level are important metrics because they allow marketers to compare it to the target demographic they have established for their brand.

Large consumer brands spend lots of time and money on research to define their audience, and if yours doesn't match their findings, the results of working together most likely won't be successful.

It is not only the brand's responsibility to make sure your audience is aligned with their product. It should be your priority as the owner of your online brand to make sure that whatever it is you decide to promote on your platform is suitable for your followers. This is the main reason some of the influencer marketing campaigns get some backlash. When there is no match between the audience and the promoted product – people get the feeling that you are selling out.

When your audience positively responds to the product you promote, it's a win-win for you and the brand. Take your time to get to know your audience.

Defining your audience in detail is not only an important exercise for you as a business owner, but it is also extremely helpful to your potential clients. Even better, if you can provide charts and metrics, verified by a third party service that specializes in audience demographics.

The most common example of such a service would be Google Analytics, which provides a line of code that you install on your blog enabling them to collect and analyze your data. In Google reports, you can find out everything from your readers' location to what kind of keywords they searched for in order to find you. However, it lacks the personal attributes of your audience, such as age and income level. These types of data can be supplemented by a service like Quantcast, which works similarly to Google Analytics. Some of the social platforms are able to provide all of this data as part of their dashboard as well.

It's worth collecting all the data you can and analyzing it together so that you can come up with a profile of your typical follower. It will help you shape your content, and most importantly, will do a huge service to the brands who are interested in working with you.

Data is the best selling tool when it comes to digital business, so add it to your arsenal.

29

MAKE A LIST OF DREAM CLIENTS

Now that you've defined your audience for potential clients, think about your side – what kind of brands would you like to work with?

If your answer is "whoever pays most," you are in the wrong business and most likely won't be able to build longevity in your influencer career. Your ideal list of brands should include companies you are genuinely excited about working with, regardless of their budgets.

Like for many businesses, your client list should be a combination of large, well-known mass brands, some boutique niche brands you have a special affinity for, and some brands that are new and need your expertise to help bring them to market.

From a financial perspective, it is important to have long-term clients who can pay your bills. However, they must be aligned with your audience. There is an advantage to working with a certain brand consistently because the connection seems more genuine to your followers. They start associating you as a natural brand ambassador and trust your opinion. After all, why would you work with this brand for a long time if you didn't believe in its product benefits?

From a brand perspective building a relationship with a particular influencer and maintaining them throughout a year, whether through paid campaigns or just product samples, is the best strategy that pays off even more over time. Creating a genuine brand ambassador takes work and, unfortunately, not many brands make the time to invest in these relationships. Sometimes it's on you to make sure it's continuing, by sending quick updates or simply reiterating how valuable you found your collaboration to be. Your clients will always appreciate any feedback you can give.

Don't be afraid to be proactive when it comes to your client relationship. You obviously don't want to be a pest, constantly following up with a client and asking when the next project comes, but staying on their radar is extremely important at times when the influencer market becomes so competitive.

From my personal experience, I rarely see influencers following up a few months later to express their interest in a next season campaign with a brand we connected them with. It always seems that they move on to the next brand that is chasing them at the moment, and in some cases, it's true. However, I can't tell you how flattered clients are to hear that a certain influencer specifically mentioned how excited they are for another opportunity to work together. We always share this info with our clients, and in most cases, if they have a budget and opportunity, they would hire that influencer again and again.

Cultivate your tight list of favorite clients and make sure they know how important they are to you.

What about dream clients you've always wanted to work with but don't know how to approach? The easiest way to get on their radar is to start including them in your editorial content. Follow their news and product releases and start mentioning the brand in your content. If the product is too pricey for you to buy on your own, reach out to their public relations department and ask for samples. Often PR relationships lead to paid opportunities, even if it takes a while.

If you want things to happen faster, you have to be proactive. Find out who your dream brand currently works with by searching the brand name on social platforms with a hashtag #ad or #sponsored. Most large companies these days utilize an influencer marketing agency or another type of agency to work with influencers. Search trade publications for mentions of their campaigns and see which agency is credited for it. It takes a bit of research to find the right contact, and a few of your emails will probably go unanswered, however, if you ask the right questions, someone will eventually guide you in the right direction.

Your goal should be working with brands you love, and you should never compromise on those with whom you associate yourself.

30

MEASURE YOURSELF
AGAINST YOUR GOALS

When you work for yourself and by yourself, how do you know whether you are doing well or struggling to get your business off the ground? And what does "doing well" even mean?

We are born with various levels of ambition and a different scale for success. For some, getting to a place where you can pay your rent and bills with the revenue you make as an influencer may symbolize success. For another, it's the jet-setting lifestyle of an influencer that makes them feel successful. For someone else, it's the notice of magazines and media that makes them feel like they have made it, while another person may not feel they've succeeded until they can buy their dream house.

These are all ambitious goals that often represent the end result, but most journeys are paved with small victories and successes that show you are on the right path. In order to maintain a healthy perspective on your career and avoid unrealistic expectations and frustration, you must establish smaller goals and milestones so you can measure yourself against them.

This is the only way to know if you are progressing in the right direction. It could be a certain audience size you hope to grow through your content, or a short list of dream brands you hope to build a relationship with, or a monthly revenue goal you hope to achieve by a certain date. Once you establish these goals and define a timeline for achieving them, you must hold yourself accountable.

This might be the hardest part because we often become delusional about our skills and chances for success. Our mind is very creative when it comes to excuses why certain things didn't work out or why certain goals were hard to achieve. We tend to give ourselves more time and chances, often losing sight of the larger aim and realizing we might be moving in a wrong direction.

On the flip side, some people never take the time to appreciate everything they have achieved, which puts them in a constant state of frustration and often leads to jealousy of others.

Setting goals and having frequent and honest check-ins with yourself about your progress will save you from taking the wrong path and allow you to adjust quickly.

31

GET OBSESSED WITH ANALYTICS

One of the great ways to measure your success is by identifying metrics that help you achieve a certain goal, and watching these metrics over time. This way you can measure the growth rate and get a clear idea whether it's consistent and try to find out what causes it to grow.

For example, if one of your goals is increasing your audience size, find online tools that allow you to see your following's growth across various social networks easily. Plenty of free tools that can quickly show you beautiful and easy to read charts are just one search away.

You can also watch these metrics easily by creating a simple spreadsheet with your numbers and updating it weekly or monthly. The advantage of doing so manually is the option of adding notes and keeping track of certain tactics so that you can analyze them later. Perhaps one day you mentioned another influencer in your post and that person returned a favor, which resulted in a small spike. This was clearly a successful tactic worth repeating. By noting it in your simple tracking system, you can later identify the cause of the spike and replicate it.

If your goal is establishing relationships with a certain number of brands, keep track of your inbound emails and see how many of them come in from brands and what causes these inquiries to surge. Is it a particular sort of content you are publishing? Hashtags you are using, or events you are attending? Perhaps you can start asking clients how they found you or what lead them to your channel. This will help you identify most successful tactics. You have to find out what drives the most inbound inquiries and continue working on it.

Analytics don't have to be complicated to give insight and help you grow. It's all about knowing what metrics are important and consistently tracking them, whether manually or through an online service.

The same methods of measurement apply to your revenue growth. You have to identify the most profitable channels and focus your energy there. Analyze each of your income streams based on the time and resources you invest in it, and then compare it to the revenue it produces. Analyze the growth of the channel – is it growing quickly or has it reached its maximum potential and plateaued? This way you can quickly see which channels to keep and which to eliminate. As a one-person show, you have to stay focused on your top-earning services. Analytics help you stay focused.

No matter how creative and artistic your personality type is, you have to develop the analytical side if you want to succeed in the digital industry. Unlike any other industries, digital marketing is driven largely by numbers, and by measuring your influence and growth you will be staying on top of performance and putting yourself ahead of the competition.

32

WORK ON YOUR WORK ETHIC

One of the best ways to continue to grow your revenue is booking repeat business. Ideally, every new client you book comes back to work with you again and again. Even if it's once a year. As you add new clients to the mix, and they all come back with frequency, that's when you see your business growing.

How do you make clients come back? Obviously, generating results is crucial, but sometimes hard to measure, depending on the services you provide. Some campaigns have a pure branding awareness nature and aren't necessarily aimed at driving sales, for example. Some have a longer-term goal and don't show measurable results until months later. Sometimes the product itself was not received well by the audience, and things are out of your control. When it comes to influencer marketing, it's often challenging to measure and prove your success.

The only thing you can control is the effort you put into your work, which defines your work ethic. If your clients see how hard you work on their behalf, they will appreciate the effort alone and always remember that, in addition to the results.

How do you prove your work ethic in the digital world when often you don't even meet or communicate with a client directly? The principles are very straightforward and similar to any job you will ever have.

First, be responsive. When it comes to online campaigns, they are often planned at the very last minute. The digital nature of our business creates the expectation of an instant turnaround and planning time is typically cut to weeks, if not days. Which means most of the opportunities you will be getting will be time-sensitive. If you don't respond to a brand's queries quickly, you may lose the opportunity because they might be reaching out to multiple people to see who they can secure the fastest. Even if that's not the case, by not responding promptly, you make the work of a person on the other end more stressful. When it comes to work pet peeves, nothing is worse than waiting for someone to respond to a time-sensitive inquiry. Not being responsive fast enough may also hurt your chances for repeat business. After all, people love working with those who make their life easier.

The second rule of great work ethic: respect the assignment and pay attention to the details, no matter how creative you would like to be. For every campaign you have been asked to work on, there were strategists and marketers that created a concept and now trust you to bring it to life. If you can't (or won't) do that, reject the opportunity. Once you agree to the assignment, there is no room for changing the details. There are reasons why you are being asked to do things in a certain way, and your piece of the puzzle might be connected to many other parts of the campaign you are not aware of. Typically, marketing initiatives have multiple pillars and can run the same messaging across TV commercials, print advertising, and influencer campaigns. All of these channels have to produce a cohesive message for a campaign to be memorable. Sometimes it's not about you and your creative expression; it's about fitting into a larger message. There will be other opportunities to collaborate with brands on something more creative, but when you are being asked to produce something specific, there is a reason behind it.

Somehow this is often why brands get frustrated working with influencers. Many influencers don't understand that they are part of a bigger initiative and have to follow direction. I can't tell you how many times during campaigns we had to go back and ask the influencer to re-shoot or re-write the content they produced because they simply didn't follow direction. It disappoints clients and leads to unnecessary delays.

This leads me to my next point: schedules are extremely important in our business. Sometimes from the influencer perspective, it may seem like it makes no difference whether the content will go live on a Thursday or Friday. However, this is not how big companies operate. Often your piece of content is part of a larger content calendar, timed with other areas of the campaign, or has a planned paid promotion behind it. Delaying your part may impact that larger project.

You also have to remember that the people on the client side report to higher ups and any delays simply make them look bad, implying they are not in control of their job. Imagine yourself in their shoes.

Do you think you would be willing to work again with a person who you put in this uncomfortable situation? Probably not.

Delays in responses and postings are probably the number one issue we see every day working with influencers. Many are simply not aware of the importance and don't prioritize timely responses, focusing mostly on the final result. They think that as long as the client is happy with the content, nothing else matters. This is a mistake that burns lots of bridges.

If you are not able to respond and accomplish assignments on time, perhaps you have to look at your to-do list and identify the cause. Is it your hectic travel schedule, or other projects you have over-committed to? Or perhaps you are just not as excited about this work and are putting it off? Be honest with yourself and reevaluate your priorities.

The worst thing you can do to your clients is drop out of the campaign completely, without a valid reason. Unfortunately, this happens more often than I'd like to admit. An influencer suddenly becomes unresponsive, or even openly tells a client that they no longer like the project after signing the contract and starting the creative process – I've seen it all. And my team has spent hours (even days) chasing influencers down and asking them to fulfill their obligations. Then, they've had to explain the situation to our clients, who were often shocked and left with a bad taste about this industry overall.

No matter how small a project may be, it contributes to your reputation as an influencer in this small industry, where word travels fast. Even if you committed to a project and regretted it later, you must fulfill your obligation. The only exception would be a change in terms that no longer fits into your content or timeline. In this case, you have the right to discuss a potential termination plan in a professional way.

Your work ethic is part of your personal brand. It might not be visible to your followers, but it is surely noted by your clients.

33

ALWAYS OVER DELIVER

Consistently delivering quality work on time is a basic rule that makes you someone people want to work with. However, if you really want to be ahead of the competition and always a top choice for brands, you have to over deliver. This holds true for any business, and what really sets you apart is great service. I'm not talking about giving away services and devaluing your work, but there are ways to make clients feel special without hurting your bottom line. Everything should be in proportion. The key is not adding on new free services, but going the extra mile with existing services you already agreed to provide.

For example, if the client requested a selection of ten photos to choose from for a project, provide fifteen or twenty. If the client sent you an extra product you love and didn't expect to receive, post a separate mention about it. If the client invited you to an expensive, all-paid trip for a photo shoot and didn't request special coverage for it, provide it anyway. This is a courtesy that doesn't cost you money. It is only a small effort, but it can go a long way.

Unfortunately, "over delivery" isn't in the vocabulary of many influencers, who refuse to do anything above the original ask. Often agents or managers block small additional requests from brands with an excuse of protecting their talent.

I've had the privilege of taking groups of influencers on incredible trips and shoots on behalf of world's most coveted brands. While in the early days these types of activations always resulted in additional organic coverage and excitement, on some of our recent trips the influencers didn't go above the obligatory scope outlined in the contract. It doesn't mean they didn't enjoy their experience or that their paid coverage wasn't incredible, but very few took that next step to over deliver and show the extra gratitude for the brands who paid for the trips, and sometimes first class tickets and five-star hotels, in addition to content fees. I see it as a missed opportunity for influencers to show how much they care about the brand they are working with and a short-sighted move that doesn't guarantee repeat business.

On the other hand, I have several examples of influencers who were smart enough to add a little extra promotion to their paid content and left a great impression on a client. In one instance, the influencer genuinely fell in love with the product she was promoting and kept talking about it way after the promotion was over. This meant that we created a true brand advocate, someone influential who is now an organic customer of the brand. It played a huge role the next time the brand considered influencers for another campaign. That influencer was on the list before anyone else!

Of course, you can't fake your love for products, but adding an extra snap or Instagram story to your promotion is an easy way to show a client how much you care.

To me, over delivering is showing your gratitude for the business, no matter what kind of services you provide or whether you are an individual or a company. "Over delivery and exceptional service" was always our motto at Style Coalition, and we go above and beyond for our clients, no matter how difficult it is to do sometimes. This is one of the reasons our clients tell us they come back, so we've proven that providing extra value doesn't hurt the business – rather, it guarantees you get repeat opportunities.

If fulfilling a special request or providing an added value coverage doesn't cost you time and money and doesn't conflict with other projects, my best advice would be to try your best to accommodate it. After all, this might be the thing that sets you apart from others and lands you your next project. In this competitive environment, when new influencers join the marketplace every day, you have to build your reputation as someone who always delivers above and beyond.

34

MAKE OTHERS SELL FOR YOU

As an influencer, you are probably wearing many different hats, and all of them demand various skills and most importantly, your attention. With time, you should work on outsourcing these hats to experts, until you find yourself in a position where you personally only handle the important creative aspects of your brand.

One of the hats that could (and should) be outsourced as early as possible is advertising sales. The main reason for that is you must separate the "church and state" of your business. As a creative professional emotionally invested in your work, most likely you will not sell your services as effectively as someone who is a seasoned sales professional or a company that specializes in this type of service.

When another party presents you to a potential advertiser, they seem more objective and can find new ways to highlight your assets from an angle you didn't think of. They are also able to negotiate better rates on your behalf because they are exposed to the wider marketplace and have a better understanding of the average rates for an influencer of your caliber.

How do you find someone who can sell for you? Luckily, there are many companies that can do it purely on a commission basis, provided they value your brand and are willing to invest resources in your sales.

Advertising networks are one example of these types of companies. Typically, they will offer to take over your display media sales if your blog has decent traffic volume. Some of these networks might bring you branded content sponsorships, along with banner ads.

The only issue is the challenging state of ad networks in the recent years, due to most advertisers switching to a programmatic sales business model. They automated most of the process by creating marketplaces for ads, public or private. Accessing a marketplace requires a relatively high minimum of monthly page views, which most influencer blogs don't reach. There are still a few companies that sell premium display ads and run niche networks, which guarantees quality, but there aren't as many as there used to be just a few years ago. You'll have to do your research on your niche and ask your peers for recommendations.

Another option would be signing up on one of the influencer marketing platforms. This way your profile would appear in their database, which is accessible to brands. Brands typically pay a subscription to access these databases, and may reach out to you directly or through the platform with paid opportunities.

There are companies, like Style Coalition, which I founded, that provide a range of opportunities – display media, as well as sponsored content and brand ambassador programs. In fact, we are known for our holistic approach to influencer marketing, which includes any type of media. We've placed influencers in print and TV ads, produced video and photo shoots for brands, put together branded events, sold banner ads, and sometimes did all of the above in one campaign.

Our process of signing influencers is pretty simple – we look for people who would be appealing to our clients and sign them up on our platform, so they become part of our database. Our goal is also to bring value to influencers, and with this approach, we've helped to build many careers. We are more selective than mass influencer platforms, simply because our clients demand higher minimums in terms of influencer reach for the type of programs we are creating. However, once you are accepted into the network and become part of our internal database, you will be proactively pitched to top brands.

Most of the networks or platforms described above do not require a long-term commitment or exclusivity on your part, which makes it easy to try a few and see what works for you.

Of course, another option is a personal manager or a talent agent, who will proactively pitch you to brands. More on that in the next chapter.

No matter who you select to handle your sales, you must form these partnerships in order to grow. You need to have people out there actively promoting your brand and bringing you opportunities. On the bright side, this is one area where you don't have to invest because most of these companies provide these services to influencers free of charge and only make their commission once they sell something.

The key is to find the right partners that fit your brand. It might take some work and research, but once you've found them, the opportunities should start coming your way. Note that you have to give each partner at least several months of trial, before you make your verdict. Most digital campaigns have a lead time of three to six months, so expecting immediate results would be unrealistic.

Finding the right network to belong to can build your career, so choose wisely!

35

DECIDE IF A MANAGER OR AGENT IS RIGHT FOR YOU

It's been several years since influencer agents popped up in the marketplace, and now they represent a big part of the industry. In addition to the new digital agents, now any traditional talent agency also has a division managing social media stars.

Most of the traditional talent agencies have a very high bar for entry, which typically requires millions of followers across social platforms. While some of the smaller agencies might be open to representing influencers with just a few hundreds or thousands of followers, it often depends on how much they believe in your brand and its so-called marketability. Since agents make their profit only from signed deals, they would hesitate to take on talent that won't produce revenue for the company over time.

The main difference between influencer networks that represent you and talent agents is that your relationships with an agent, in most cases, would be exclusive. That means every inquiry you receive from

a brand must be routed to the agent for vetting, nego-
tiating, and signing on your behalf. Therefore, agents
typically represent just a handful of influencers. Depending on your individual contract, they are obli-
gated to explore every deal that comes your way,
which results in quite a lot of work. It is in their pri-
mary interest to get you the highest paying job and
make sure that job doesn't conflict or prevent you
from getting other work.

As you can see, an agent plays a major role in
your career and often has the power and authority to
decline opportunities that you would be willing to accept on your own. This makes the decision of signing
with an agent that shares your values crucial to your
success. Talent agency contracts are typically long-
term and binding when it comes to many important
issues. Therefore, you should never sign one without
consulting an attorney that has expertise in talent rep-
resentation.

As a rule of thumb, your contract with the talent agency should never be one-sided. You have to ask
what the agent would do for you in return for you signing off your exclusivity for the next few years. Your expectations need to be aligned for the relationship to
succeed. No one will be able to guarantee you revenue;
however, you should agree on the rates the agent will
be presenting to brands on your behalf. You also
should be able to request to review all opportunities
before they get accepted or rejected. Ideally, you will
always have the final word, even if the agent thinks the
opportunity is not worthwhile.

Most importantly, you need to have a clear
idea of how the agent will be positioning you to clients

and helping you grow your brand. You have to under-stand what their strengths are – is it social media-only deals, product licensing, book deals, TV appearances or anything else that can help you build your empire? Not all agents specialize in everything, so you need to make sure the most important items on your list fall under their expertise. In some cases, you might be able to get two different agents handling various as-pects of your business, or limit their exclusivity only to the area you need help with the most. For example, your agent might be managing anything related to speaking, TV appearances, and book deals, but you might be able to sell digital-only campaigns on your own as well.

In some instances, when you have existing long-term relationship with a brand, you might be able to carve out that client from your agent's contract. It might be smart for you to continue managing your most important clients, who are used to working with you directly. Adding an agent to the mix might create more work on the client's end, not to mention increase the rate they are paying.

This leads me to the next point: make sure you and your agent are on the same page regarding your rates increase. During my work with influencers who grow fast and get signed by an agent, I've seen the rates for an individual influencer jump to triple or quadruple what they used to be in a matter of just a few months. While that influencer might have under-charged previously, in most cases these rate increases are hard to justify to clients.

Ask your potential agent lots of questions, and pay attention to any red flags, such as over-promises, vague terms, or simply someone who is trying to steer you in a direction that does not align with your beliefs.

Another route you may choose at some point in your career is hiring a personal manager who, as opposed to an agent, will be working for you and you alone, and will protect your interests as their full-time job. Being able to afford a personal manager is typically a step most influencers can take only later in their career, but it can certainly pay off and put you in control of your destiny.

In the meantime, once you start building your team, one of the members may be able to act as a manager and vet opportunities and inquiries on your behalf. All you need is someone smart and professional, who is able to communicate effectively with prospects. You will need to establish rules and guide them along the way, but this will enable you to control your deals better and utilize team members more efficiently. In this entrepreneurial world, everyone has to multitask!

Working with agents and managers for years, I've seen all kinds of people fulfilling this role – from an influencer's own mom to a former Hollywood shark. No matter who the person may be, they have to represent you in the best light possible because most of the time they will be the client-facing person. They must be responsive, polite, efficient, and organized. They must know you well and help you prioritize the opportunities that would be most beneficial to your career. Most importantly, you have to be able to trust them.

36

MANAGE YOUR RATES

Since the early days, influencer rates have been a subject of controversy in the press and media. Most of the coverage you can find on the subject has a negative stigma attached to influencers demanding unreasonable prices for their services, which are often impossible to quantify.

There are several reasons for the controversy, and some of them are understandable. First, it's a new industry that doesn't have a long history, proper rules, or regulations. The rates are mostly defined by individuals according to their subjective view of their own value.

Another reason is the high demand for certain individual influencers at the top tier level that inflates some of their rates. For example, if an influencer can produce only four sponsored posts in a month, but has inquiries from eight brands, their solution is often raising their rates. This is an understandable reaction in a free market. However, it does put off many of the brands that can no longer afford that influencer. Too many times, we've had an established working relationship with an influencer and a go-to rate, only to find out one day that the rate has tripled because of their high demand. Unfortunately, these situations result not only in a brand never coming back to that influencer, but getting a bad impression of the influencer space overall.

Expansion of the influencer pool is helping with this short-term situation, as more individuals become power influencers and, therefore, offer brands more options of people to work with.

Perhaps the largest cause of skepticism when it comes to influencer rates is the lack of proof that influencers drive ROI (Return on Investment). While there are multiple reports online claiming as much as a tenfold return on every dollar spent on influencer marketing, these reports are mostly produced by the influencer platforms or agencies, who lack an objective point of view on the subject. As of 2016, there hasn't been large-scale research done by a reputable independent source to verify this data.

Most brands rely on a measurement of clicks received from an influencer's content and the number of sales generated from these clicks. This straightforward approach works for programs that drive specific product promotion and sales, however many influencer marketing programs are aimed at brand awareness, and product purchase is not necessarily immediate. Consumers may be inspired to try a product in a store after seeing it on an influencer's Instagram. In this case, there is no way to register a connection between that sale and the influencer. Brands can measure an overall lift in sales following their influencer marketing program, but there could be other factors involved, and the connection could be hard to prove.

How does this affect your rates as an influencer? Very much, because brands look at their marketing spend from an ROI perspective, and if they can't justify spending part of their budget on your fee or are having a hard time quantifying your value – they won't be risking it.

Therefore, your rates should be based on other factors besides demand so that you can build real value for your brand partners. Your history of performance plays an important role here, and any data you can provide to a potential client, such as sales, leads, or engagement generated would be crucial to defining how much they are willing to spend on a partnership with you.

Other important factors in establishing your rates are the value of your content and how the brand is planning to utilize it for their purposes. For example, if you are asked to create a short video that will be used on brand's website with your name attached to it, you are creating valuable content that a brand would otherwise be paying someone else to create. So, it's important to understand how your content or collaboration would be used, which may drive the rates up or down.

As an up and coming influencer, you may view a feature on a brand's website as an added value to you because it's promoting your brand and helps you book more campaigns with others. For that reason, you may want to provide a discounted rate for this type of project. However, as an established influencer, you may look at the same situation as an opportunity to charge more, since the brand will be using your name and image to promote their products. This might limit your ability to work with competitive brands at the same time, so you would want to be compensated for that potential loss. It just goes to show you that rates should stay flexible and be adjusted based on your career stage and demand, as well as the overall market situation.

You don't want to alienate brands you are passionate about from working with you because they can no longer afford you. Often your dream brands will be those with a smaller budget but the most prestige, so be aware of that and know when to discount.

Asking for a high rate puts more pressure on you to deliver and holds you to a high standard. If you can't deliver the value a brand expects for the budget they spent, they likely won't hire you again, which may shorten your career as an influencer.

Best practice, in the beginning, would be to see what rates the market is willing to offer for your services and build a steady book of clients who are coming back.

Raising your rates should always be a gradual process, something you are building up as you grow and prove your value to more and more clients. If you choose to negotiate a rate you've been offered, always ask if there is room to do so first; don't assume people have an unlimited budget or will try to take advantage of you. Be prepared to defend your request for more money or explain the increase.

On your rapid growth path, don't forget the clients who supported you early on. Give them a special rate that will make them feel like part of your journey. It's good karma and a good business practice. Some relationships are hard to put a value on, so don't forget that when you get to the top.

37

CREATE DEMAND

One of the best ways to guarantee your rates will be accepted is to create demand. When your services are in demand, you have control over who you work with and how much you charge them. Of course, creating demand isn't an easy task; it requires strategy, persistence and, most importantly, action.

As an influencer, you have to put yourself out there to attract clients. This could be done in a variety of ways. Your content is one of the easiest and most organic ways to do so. Besides creating great quality content, organically mentioning relevant brands gets their attention. Most brands use various services that notify them of organic coverage, whether it's on the web or social platforms. They monitor all mentions and highlight the most notable. Of course, this must be an authentic practice that is done in moderation and only when it's truly relevant to the piece of content and your readers. If you start mentioning brands for the sake of being noticed, both your followers and the brand might start questioning your motives.

Another way to get noticed is through publicity and traditional press. Use these opportunities to attract potential clients, and invest time and effort in submitting your blog for various awards and competitions. You may even try pitching your content to traditional publications, such as magazines and their online properties. They're always looking for original content to feature, so you could be in luck.

Attending industry events and covering them via dedicated hashtags on social platforms often places you on the map not only with the brands sponsoring these events, but also with their competitors, who often follow the coverage.

Lastly, producing great work for other brands attracts more clients who can clearly see your value. Brands feel more comfortable hiring you when they know that you've done this before and understand the rules of the game. It is helpful to participate in campaigns with multiple influencers, especially well-known ones, because these campaigns often get more attention overall. Plus, your name will be on the list with some of your successful peers, which is a great affiliation. It is worth considering participation in those campaigns even at lower rates, particularly at the beginning, because they contribute to your positioning as an influencer.

All of these tactics are helpful in creating demand for your services, and they allow you to focus only on landing paid opportunities and getting into the luxurious position of being able to decline anything that doesn't fit with your brand or your rates.

38

DIVERSIFY YOUR REVENUE CHANNELS

As your business grows and becomes your source of income, it is important to protect yourself by diversifying your revenue channels.

While collaborations with brands are a great source of revenue (and is the most creative one by far), the timing of these opportunities is often unpredictable. Most brands have a seasonal marketing strategy that may depend on certain holidays or product launches. For example, most retailers spend the bulk of their budget in the fourth quarter, targeting Christmas shoppers. Most beauty brands plan around new product releases, which change from brand to brand. Some products could have seasonal consumption, which will affect the brand's marketing spend as well. All of this means that branded content opportunities may come your way inconsistently, and some months might be slower than others.

By diversifying your revenue channels, you help create some consistency in your revenue stream.

If things slow down in one area, you can count on the other channels to supplement your total income.

In this fast-paced digital space, things change constantly. For example, banner ads used to be a major source of income for many bloggers just a few years ago. Since then programmatic technologies entered the space, automated most campaigns, and thus drove the rates down. Most bloggers now get just a fraction of the revenue they used to get, and have to come up with alternative revenue sources. Those who had diverse revenue channels were in a better position once things started to change.

Another reason to diversify is to reduce the risk of running out of money if, for example, one client doesn't pay on time. Some big corporations have very slow payment processes, and some things fall between the cracks unintentionally. If this happens consistently with a specific client, you may want to establish some ground rules. However, you will be running the risk of not being selected to work with this client again if flexibility with payment terms is important to them. It is a good rule to make sure you are not dependent on one client for more than a quarter of your monthly revenue. This way you can cover most of your expenses, even if one big client is late.

How do you create diversity in your revenue streams if all you sell is your influence? Think about which parts of your brand you can monetize, and find partners who can help grow these revenue streams.

For instance, the advertising space on your blog can be handled by an ad network, which creates a monthly revenue stream. Your YouTube ad space could be managed by an MCN (multi-channel network) that specializes in monetizing video. Your agent or manager can handle your social activations. You may have a direct relationship with a long-standing client for hosting their events, which serves as another stream. If you publish a book or collaborate with a brand on a line of products, this will result in royalties. If you create your own products, the profits are all yours.

All these revenue streams, big or small, add up to your total income and provide a certain level of stability and consistency, which are necessary for any business. It allows you not to depend on one channel. The next step is to keep optimizing each of these streams, so your total revenue continues to grow.

39

AUTOMATE REVENUE CHANNELS

Creating multiple revenue channels and keeping up with all of them may sound overwhelming at first. However, the key is to automate each, so they take the minimum amount of management on your part.

Royalties are a great example of an automated revenue stream that doesn't require any work on your part, except the initial effort of creating a product.

Books are a great tool for creating such revenue, and with the advanced self-publishing tools we have today, all you have to do is upload your file to Amazon and watch the royalties deposited every month to your bank account. Companies like CreateSpace automate the entire process for independent authors, and make it easy for anyone to get published without any initial investment, besides your time and the effort of writing the manuscript. With the audience you have built, and a small promotional push, you can start generating monthly revenue right away.

Of course, you may also choose the route of traditional book publishing, but unless you have an agent who is willing to pitch you to book publishers, or have a publisher approaching you, the process may take years and eventually yield fewer royalties than a self-published book. Most of the deals for first-time authors provide only a small advance and a much smaller percentage of royalties than a self-published book. On top of that, most publishers would expect you to do most of the promotion, which reduces the value they provide these days, compared to self-publishing.

Banner advertising is another great example of an automated revenue stream. All it takes is selecting an advertising network partner, installing their tags, and letting them sell ads for you. Most of the networks will be willing to help with the technical aspects of the initial setup, and will provide monthly reports or even a real-time performance dashboard for the ads they sell on your site.

Some networks will work with you month-to-month, while others may require a longer commitment. Before you sign any exclusive contracts, make sure the network is willing to provide a certain percentage of guaranteed sell-through, as well as minimum rates. Ideally, you will be able to get out of the commitment with a termination notice, which can range from thirty to ninety days. When it comes to advertising networks, many often overpromise, so it's important to establish a test period or find a trusted partner recommended by other influencers.

Affiliate networks that pay commissions on products sold from your links are a great revenue channel because your content may continue to bring revenue long after it's posted, assuming the recommended product is still available. With a little initial setup and some research into what products yield the most revenue, this is a great way to monetize your audience – as long as people actually listen to your recommendations and buy the product.

Affiliate marketing may take up lots of your time in the beginning, but once you learn what works for your audience, the process should be pretty automatic. The key is to find the right network (or a few) for different types of products. You can sign up for one of the generic networks, like LinkShare or Amazon. However you may see a higher commission percentage with niche networks that specialize in your category. For example, rewardStyle may work best for fashion products. Some retailers even have direct affiliate marketing programs accessible to top influencers.

There is no one formula that fits all when it comes to product recommendations. It all depends on your type of content and your specific audience. The best approach is to try working with several networks, and tag various types of products and price points to see what performs best. Spend some time on reports and analytics, watching how each affiliate link performs – what types of products get the most clicks, most purchases, and who are the retailers that pay the most commission. Analyze the results and establish a strategy that you can easily follow without being overwhelmed by the many options. When done right, affiliate marketing typically becomes one of the largest revenue channels for influencers. Those who cracked the code on what works for their audience, see tremendous returns.

Content licensing is a new revenue channel that my company Style Coalition is pioneering this year. The idea behind it is to allow online content creators – Instagrammers and bloggers – to license their editorial content for marketing campaigns. Many lifestyle influencers create amazing content on a daily basis, and only a small percentage of it is sponsored and monetized. What about all the gorgeous photos that end up posted once and never looked at again? That's what our new platform, called ContentExchange, is offering to brands. From a brand perspective, they pay a lower fee for licensing versus creating something original, and save the time it takes to produce. I believe this new automated revenue channel will become significant for any lifestyle influencer.

Bottom line: anything that only requires an initial time investment and continues to bring revenue over time is a great source of income, and you should strive not only to create those channels but to automate them to the point where they require very minimal time spent on your part. Your time is money, and you have to invest it in larger deals.

40

CREATE TANGIBLE PRODUCTS

One of the greatest ways to create additional revenue channels, besides the typical digital formats, is to produce physical products and sell them to your audience. Having your name on a product also adds cachet to your brand, making you appear as a multi-channel business.

When coming up with product ideas, it's best to start simple and create something your audience already buys. It is also important to keep it authentic to your existing content. For example, if you are a style influencer who is known for your exceptional taste in jewelry, creating your own jewelry line is a natural extension of your brand and your business. Your readers, who trust your taste and resonate with your style, might be much more inclined to buy the jewelry from you than from another emerging designer with whom they don't have the same personal connection. Buying a product is not only about the purchase, but it's also about supporting with your wallet the people and brands you care about. Hopefully, the audience you have built has a genuine connection with you and will be willing to support your new venture.

The key is to make sure your products meet your standard and truly represent who you are. You must be careful in selecting the right partners when it comes to production, materials, packaging, and everything else that goes into the consumer experience. Remember, your product is an extension of your brand.

Creating physical products isn't an easy task; it often requires investment. It is typically accessible to influencers at a later stage, those who have built a significant brand and are able to invest in creating a line. How can an emerging influencer take advantage of their own products? A great way to start is collaborating with an existing brand that already produces the type of product you wish to create. This way, they are only licensing your name and incorporating your design ideas, but they're taking care of everything else – manufacturing, packaging, shipping, compliances, and approvals. Even though the returns are not as high in these kinds of licensing deals as they would be with your own line of products, the point of entry is much easier because it doesn't require your own investment. It also allows you to test your audience, and determine whether they are even interested in this type of product from you.

Whatever route you choose, licensing or manufacturing, you will be adding an additional revenue channel to your business. Instead of recommending products created by others and earning an affiliate commission on it, you will be selling your own products and generating a much higher fee. Ideally you would find a manufacturer or a company that can handle the logistics for you, so you can focus on the creative aspects of this venture. This is another area where a good agent or manager can help you research and connect with the right people.

Your own line of products not only adds to your diverse revenue stream, it also helps to monetize your audience in various ways. Take each reader of your blog, and look at the ways they could potentially produce revenue for you – they view advertisements on your page, they read your sponsored posts, they click on your affiliate links, and finally, they buy products you have created. By utilizing all these revenue streams, you will be able to get a much higher return per audience member. Think of it from a business perspective: how much revenue could each follower produce for you? Aim to increase that number year over year, by adding new products they can consume.

41

MANAGE YOUR CASH FLOW

With all the various revenue streams, expenses and areas that you invest in, the most important thing for your business is cash flow – money coming in and out. Most people believe that businesses fail because of the idea or execution, but I believe businesses fail because of poor cash flow management. Money is the fuel for your business, and if the fuel is not flowing properly, you won't have a chance to try new ideas or improve your execution.

Once you have established your core revenue channels, and hopefully automated some of them, you should have a good idea of your average monthly income. I suggest building out an annual projection of your income, divided by months and how much you expect each revenue channel to bring. Find the balance between conservative and optimistic estimates. Use existing metrics to account for growth. For example, if your revenue has been growing by five percent each month for several months, it's a pattern that points to consistent growth. You can use this assumption to estimate your future revenue growth.

You should also keep a good record of your business expenses – anything from your website's hosting bill to travel and wardrobe, if these relate to a professional project.

The goal of the cash flow spreadsheet is to balance out at the end of each month and generate profit that covers your non-business expenses and leaves some room for savings.

The cash flow document is never set in stone, and is more of a working document that you can adjust as you go. It also makes you accountable for your income and spending.

While it's important to stay optimistic with your projections, you have to stay grounded and remember that events outside of your control may often affect your income. Industry trends change, advertisers cut their budgets or don't always pay on time, that's why you always have to protect yourself and leave a certain percentage of your profits in savings.

With that said, it is also good to explore your credit options, which will allow you to weather the tough times until you build a more consistent revenue stream or invest in important areas of your business. Some banks are able to offer a small business credit line, or you may look into one of the online lenders who may charge higher interest but make the lending process easier. Make sure you are capable of paying off these loans before you take them on, as most will require a personal guarantee. I would suggest using this option only against signed contracts or guaranteed future revenue, so you don't expose yourself financially.

Most importantly, be disciplined in managing your finances. Pace yourself with big spending until your business is more established and you have consistent and repeat sources of revenue. Otherwise, the financial stress can take a toll on your creativity, which is one of the most dangerous things you can do to yourself as a content creator.

42

STAY ON TOP OF MONEY COLLECTION

One of the most important things for a positive cash flow is timely money collection. It gets challenging to keep up with invoices once you have multiple revenue streams; however, you should allocate some time every month to go over your outstanding payments, and follow up with these partners. Even if you have a manager or a bookkeeper, you still have to review the pipeline of paid projects and make sure you are properly and timely compensated. This is one of the things a business owner has to stay involved in personally, no matter how big or small your company may be.

Collecting money probably won't be your favorite part of the business. Many creative people feel shy when talking about money. Or worse, they become emotional, and use a language that comes off as too aggressive. Money is indeed a sensitive subject when it comes to the creative arts. It gets especially touchy when you, the creator, are not able to outsource this task to an agent or a manager, and have to negotiate and then chase the money yourself. Here are a few important tips you need to know when collecting money:

Make sure you have the right contact – the person who oversees payments. If your contact is a marketing person, ask to get connected to someone at the accounting department so you can keep your relationship "clean" from the payments talk.

Before you follow up to demand payment, re-read your contract to make sure you have the right information regarding payment timing and terms. Following up on a payment before it's due will only annoy the other party. However, there is nothing wrong with reaching out in advance to ask whether you can expect the payment on time.

If the payment is delayed, try to get to the bottom of it and find out why. Was the client happy with your work? Provide numbers to support your performance to make sure. Do they have all the info they need to pay you? Often companies will ask for invoices, as well as necessary tax forms and updated address info. Will they be paying by check, wire transfer, or using one of the online services to send you money? Make sure you are aware of the processing times of the chosen payment method.

It is important to understand a company's payment process. Often, you will be working with a client through their agency, and won't be receiving payment until the client pays the agency. There isn't much you can do in this situation, aside from following up once in a while and staying on their radar. Most likely, the agency wants to get paid as much as you do, and they are doing their best to secure the funds. Unfortunately, this happens very often in the digital marketing industry, and you should not see it as out of the ordinary or worry about whether you will get paid at all. If the brand is a trusted company with a proven track record, they will eventually pay. Until then, you have to keep your cool. Stay persistent but polite.

I can't tell you how many times I've seen people burn bridges by being unprofessional in handling payment inquiries. Unless you have proof that the other side is lying to you and holding back your money, you have to stay patient and believe that everyone has the best intentions to pay you.

Being a business owner is not an easy task (even if your business consists of just yourself), and you must be prepared for times when your funds will be delayed. In fact, you should be prepared for a number of delays, and have a plan B that allows you to have financial freedom and not stress about every check while you wait for it. Financial issues create unnecessary stress, which takes your energy away from the creative side of the business.

Be smart about not only making money but also managing it properly, so you never have to lose relationships over it.

PART 4:
MANAGE YOUR
SUCCESS

43

EDUCATE YOURSELF ABOUT THE INDUSTRY

Once you start getting clients and working with brands in various capacities, you technically become part of the online marketing industry. You now work in influencer marketing – one of the newest and hottest marketing channels, which launched only a few years ago. Whether you want to or not, you must have some knowledge about the industry to participate competently in your business transactions.

To navigate the space, you need to see how your brand fits into the large landscape of influencers, and what type of clients and campaigns you should be able to attract based on your positioning. You have to understand what brands are looking for at this very moment. You can observe other people's work, make contacts within the industry, and ask them specific questions before you start selling your services.

You also need to understand the players you are dealing with – the differences between media agencies, creative shops, production companies, influencer marketing platforms, talent agents, and public relation firms. You have to understand the roles each plays in this process. Often you will be working with all of the above on a single campaign.

For instance, you might be participating in a campaign that was initiated by a brand's media agency, conceptualized by their creative shop, produced by a production company, cast by an influencer marketing platform, managed by a talent agent, and promoted by a brand's public relations team. Each of these parties has multiple team members who have assigned roles on a project. It may sound like too many people are involved, but each has a very specific job, and certain campaigns do take a village. Typically, anything that has a six-figure budget and above will have a team of people that work with you, and you need to understand each person's title and role in order to communicate in a professional manner.

To build longevity, you need to know the trends and where the industry is going. You need to see a few steps ahead, and try to innovate among your peers. In our reality, you simply can't do the same thing for years and get comfortable. Things constantly change, trends come and go, new platforms launch, and the audience moves on to the next hot thing. To keep up with the trends, you can read leading publications on the subject or set up Google alerts for important news. Subscribing to trade publications and their daily editions or newsletters is a great way to start. Whether it's a general advertising publication like *AdAge,* or a niche outlet like *Women's Wear Daily* that covers anything retail, set aside some time each week to read relevant articles. Most importantly, you need to become part of the community, so you can be in the know before the news hits the press.

If you don't know at least the basics, you will never be able to turn your craft into a legit business, respected by your peers and valued by clients. Set aside time each week to educate yourself on these various aspects of the industry so you can become a real part of it.

44

STUDY YOUR CLIENTS

When you start working with brands, you must spend the time to get to know them. After all, they hired you to provide them with services, so get a good idea of their expectations.

You can't create branded content in a vacuum; you must do your research to get a good idea of the essence of the brand. Your services as a content creator should fit into their overall strategy, their look and feel, and their voice. That doesn't mean you need to change yours to adapt, of course. Successful creative collaborations take the best of both worlds and create something new.

Looking at their past work, especially collaborations with influencers like yourself, can inform and direct your efforts. First, you don't want to repeat something that has been done. Second, you don't want to appear amateur by not understanding the brand's values. This is especially true for premium and luxury brands. While mass, lower priced brands will be easier to satisfy, high-end brands tend to have a very specific set of dos and don'ts when it comes to content. In the online world, it's easy to find all of the above, and there is no excuse for ignorant work.

I have countless examples of working with influencers who didn't bother to read a brand's provided materials. The worst of the offenses, and it has happened way too many times, is when an influencer mispronounces a brand's name in the video content they create. There is nothing worse you can do to a brand to indicate that you have no clue who they are.

Another example would be creating content that is too risqué for a brand that is traditional in their values. This puts both the brand and the influencer in an uncomfortable situation. Before stretching your creative limits, find out how comfortable the brand is with taking a risk or challenging some perceptions.

The balance between your creative freedom and a brand's strategy is one of the hardest things to solve in influencer marketing. This is the reason there are so many agencies and middlemen who are responsible for connecting brands with influencers. That's where my company had the most success – coming up with creative ideas that allow influencers enough room for self-expression, while still sticking to the brand's objectives. If you don't work through an agency that can help you understand the boundaries, it's up to you to figure them out by asking as many questions as you can.

Why is it so important to get the brand essence right and understand your client? Because you want to establish repeat business. This is one of the most important rules of growing your business and revenue.

Constantly searching for new clients is exhausting. As a business owner, you have to aim for repeat business of at least half of your clients, and work on expanding your base from there. Knowing your clients well gives you the power to create work that satisfies them. It also gives you a good idea of their marketing strategy, planning cycle, and how often you can expect them to return.

Knowing these facts is crucial for being able to forecast your revenue and maintain a healthy cash flow. Any sales start with a relationship and, like in any good relationship, you need to know your partner.

45

GET BASIC FINANCE KNOWLEDGE

Terms like cash flow and forecasting might sound intimidating, but you must work on getting used to them to be a successful business owner. It's hard to rely on consultants to manage your finances, especially in the beginning when your resources are limited. Yes, you should get a good accountant to provide financial and tax reports, and that person might be able to advise you on some other financial issues, but they won't be able to manage your day-to-day cash or build a proper forecast of your revenue. You are the person who knows your clients well and can see some patterns in revenue coming in. You are the only one who knows when to anticipate certain opportunities, as well as keep track of all your various revenue channels.

You can (and should) outsource the monthly bookkeeping and the annual tax preparation. Often your accountant who prepares the annual taxes will be able to keep an eye on your books throughout the year to make sure you are compliant with various laws. Sometimes, even having all of the above people in place doesn't guarantee that things won't slip through the cracks.

At the end of the day, it's your responsibility as a business owner to pay taxes, purchase insurance, bill your clients, create proper contracts, understand how payroll works, and a million other things you are not aware of when working for other people.

Here again, education comes into play, and there are no excuses these days for not being able to learn the basics. Obviously, there are plenty of online resources for small business owners that can teach you the essentials, and asking your accountant for a general overview of the main accounting rules can be a good place to start. Make a habit of writing down any financial questions that may come up in your day-to-day, and schedule a monthly call with your financial advisor to address them. This way, you will be learning something new that helps you excel as a business owner every month.

Being a creative person, I can certainly relate to the struggle most creative people have with managing the financial aspects of their business. When I launched Style Coalition, I could not even afford a bookkeeper, so I decided to learn QuickBooks software and, for the first couple of years, did the bookkeeping myself. Learning to navigate the accounting software was an extremely valuable lesson because I can now easily review the work of my finance employees and communicate with them using the proper terms. At any moment, I can jump in and generate my own reports and fix urgent errors, if needed.

In order to project and analyze your revenue, you must be able to read and understand financial reports. Not to mention, if you ever decide to raise money or take a bank loan, you should be able to answer several financial questions. Some of the basics include your profit and loss statement (P&L), balance sheet, profit margin, burn rate, and operational expenses. All of these reports are typically auto-generated by your accounting software. Make it a habit to review them at least once a month and analyze some of the trends you are seeing.

Most importantly, knowing these numbers allows you to create your cash flow projections, which is the most crucial report, showing the life expectancy of your business. Your goal is to have enough resources and incoming revenue to sustain your business for at least a few months ahead. A detailed cash flow projection document allows you to see into the future and fix any potential problems before they happen. It can be as simple as a few lines outlining your expected income, expenses, and profits month by month. It might seem unnecessary in the beginning, but as your business grows, it will become more complex and absolutely essential. By creating this habit early on, your growth will be easier to manage.

Knowledge is power, and knowing your numbers puts you in charge of your business. No excuses.

46

GET BASIC LEGAL KNOWLEDGE

Just like your finances, legal is another area that you can't completely outsource without understanding at least the basics. Some matters will be too important not to consult with a lawyer, and you should have someone in your arsenal since most of your legal matters will consist of business contracts.

Unless you have an agent, it will be your job to review and negotiate your contracts. Most likely you won't be able to afford a lawyer to review every contract you will be signing, unless you have a family member or a friend who is willing to give you free advice as you grow. Most lawyers charge hundreds to thousands of dollars per hour, and some contracts are just too small to justify that kind of expense. In these cases, it will be up to you (and your manager) to read the terms and negotiate.

You have to familiarize yourself with fundamental legal terms, as you will see them repeating from contract to contract. While contracts look intimidating at first, once you understand their typical structure, it's easy to scroll through and focus on the important parts. These parts typically would be the scope of work, payment amount and payment terms, cancellation policy, usage rights, intellectual property, and responsibilities of each party.

While some legal terms are standard and exist in every contract, others are specific to content creation deals. These include usage rights, usage territories, mediums where the content can be published, and for how long the brand is able to use it. Some contracts may ask you for exclusivity during the term, which could limit your ability to work with the brand's competitors or even an entire category of brands. Clauses like these may result in increased fees, so it's important to understand the limitations that come with every contract.

It is in your best interest to have these contracts as detailed as possible, so everyone's expectations are aligned, and there are no misunderstandings about your rights or responsibilities.

If the brand gives you a product to try as part of the assignment, make sure to specify whether the product is gifted to you or consigned. Some products may cost thousands of dollars, and the brand might be willing to let you borrow them for your assignment but will expect it back at the end, and in good condition.

Another key part of the contract is the project description. It includes tactical details like the project schedule, the number of postings and editing rounds, to help keep everyone on time and budget. It protects each party in the event that things change during the project, in which case you have the right to re-negotiate the contract. It also protects you from making countless revisions according to the brand's demands.

Let's face it, most of the content is subjective, which means you might find yourself editing it over and over again because someone on the client side keeps changing their mind. Obviously, client satisfaction should be your top priority; however, you need to have the ability to refuse revisions on a project that has spiraled out of control. That's where the contract comes in to protect you.

While all these examples don't have major implications, signing on certain terms can make or break your career in some cases. For example, allowing a brand to use your content in perpetuity across their national retail locations may limit your ability to work with other competitive brands. Not specifying the mediums on which a brand can post your content allows them to publish it anywhere they want, including marketing brochures and billboards. As much as it may excite you to see yourself on a billboard, these types of details need to be negotiated upfront and charged for accordingly.

Being able to read your contracts is a crucial skill to any independent content creator. If legal language intimidates you, ask a lawyer to walk you through some of the basic terms. Then ask him or her to review with you all the potential pitfalls, so you can watch out for them and ask the right questions. This will give you the confidence to address your legal concerns on your own and make you a better business person.

47

LEARN TO NEGOTIATE

Another important skill for any entrepreneur who is in charge of their own income is the ability to negotiate. Sometimes it's even the ability to talk about money without emotional strings, which seems to be a challenge for many creative professionals. We are too attached to our work and our brand to be able to put the right price tag on it. Sometimes we overvalue ourselves, but mostly the opposite is the case.

This is where the ability to negotiate and hold your ground in a professional way comes in handy. Money is a sensitive subject for many, and can alienate existing or potential clients if not talked about carefully. The key in most negotiations is to know your value and to be able to back it up with facts. Once you know your value and truly believe in it, saying it out loud (or writing it in an email) becomes easier.

If you are not sure where you fall on the scale of influencer rates, ask a few potential clients how much they would be willing to pay for your services. Sometimes the market can give you a good indication of where you should stand. Comparing a few answers will give you a good average that you can use as a starting point.

There is no need to get offended when the compensation offered is way below your desired rate. It's never personal. Simply thank the person and walk away. In most cases, the person who is trying to "low-ball" you is forced by their client or boss to get aggressive with budgets, and it's not entirely their decision. The same person might have a larger budget for another campaign down the road, so never burn bridges.

Being able to walk away from something that isn't worth accepting is very powerful, and sends the message to those on the other side of the table. Sometimes you will be surprised, as they come back with a significantly higher budget. However, you should also understand that they may never come back. There is a way to walk away while leaving the door open, and you can master that skill.

One quality that always helps the other side to feel good about the negotiation is your gratefulness. No matter how far or close the offer is to your actual rate, be grateful that someone is willing to pay you for your services. Many brands don't have a large promotional budget, so sometimes the offer is simply all they can pay. Making them feel bad for this fact won't help you get where you want.

Practice gratitude and negotiate non-emotionally to achieve the results you want.

48

LEARN TO SAY NO

As an influencer and content creator, you will often be asked to provide all sorts of services for a variety of brands. Not all services may feel authentic to who you are for various reasons. Not all client brands will be a fit for yours, and not all will resonate with your audience.

Be careful of what you say yes to, and learn the art of saying no. This is one of the biggest issues currently polluting the influencer marketing space. Many influencers feel like their career could be short-term and, therefore, they should cash in on every deal that knocks on their door.

This is the reason you see someone promoting a luxury handbag one day and the newest fast food sandwich the day after. In some cases, ninety percent of the influencer's content is sponsored, which dilutes the value of every brand collaboration they've done. It is also very short-sighted, as the career of an influencer can last many years and evolve into other areas.

For example, someone who started as an influencer may evolve into a TV host or other industry expert. Integrity is part of your brand and is hard to repair once weakened. Accepting opportunities that cause people to question your integrity puts your brand in danger. Everything you've built can suddenly look empty of purpose and full of greed. Like with any brand damage, once you are labeled a "sell out" in the minds of your audience or potential clients, it's hard to go back.

This shows you that saying no is sometimes more important than saying yes. How do you know what's right and what's wrong to accept? Listen to your heart, and ask yourself why you are excited about a certain project. Typically, the rule of thumb is that if you are doing it only for the money, you shouldn't be doing it. Your work (and especially sponsored projects) should be fueled by passion and creativity, not monetary compensation.

It's up to you to decide how many sponsored collaborations you'll accept in a certain period, but it is recommended that no more than twenty percent of your total content should be sponsored. If you go above that, you need to make sure your brand partnerships are truly organic, and the type of content you create for them is very similar to your editorial coverage. This way your followers will feel like they are still getting the content they came to consume. Carefully selecting your projects will keep you authentic, and limiting paid collaborations will show your followers that you are not in it for the money alone.

For every opportunity that comes your way, think about whether you would be proud of the work you would do with it. Sometimes saying no opens the possibility for something bigger and better.

49

LEARN TO HIRE

As an entrepreneur, you are always faced with decisions, so it's important to surround yourself with the right people who can help you make the right choices and guide you in the right direction. Your photographer, your assistant, your manager, accountant, and lawyer – all these people could be a part of your team once you succeed in turning your craft from a one-person show into a business.

To build this team of professionals, you must learn how to hire. We talked about all the skills you need to become successful, from financial knowledge to legal, but Human Resources might be most important of all. The people that you surround yourself with can deeply affect your career. Being careful of who you let into your inner circle of trust is crucial. One unprofessional employee or teammate can damage your business and reputation. On the opposite end, someone who is loyal and believes in you can help you grow faster, by providing the daily positive support and taking over professional tasks.

You must surround yourself with people who not only possess the knowledge you need, but also believe in you and are willing to be honest and loyal.

I've made my share of hiring mistakes, and as much as I try to learn from them, most are subjective to a particular individual. Each person you get to work with represents huge potential, but also a challenge – for some people it may be different communication styles, for others it's providing and receiving feedback. It's impossible to find a perfect fit, and the list of your "must-haves" may be different from role to role. While it's important for your client-facing manager to have great service skills, it would be not as crucial for your accountant.

Another challenge is getting to know the person you are considering for a job in a short period of time, and without testing out their work. This is where working with professional service providers who charge by the hour or by day is way easier than hiring an employee. With service providers, you can easily switch to a different one if things are not working. With employees, the ties are harder to break. That's why you have to be extra careful with your hires and the terms you sign.

How do you know who to choose as your partners in this adventure? One thing that has worked well for me is listening very carefully to a candidate's answers, paying attention to anything that raises a red flag – especially when their initial likability is established. We often tend to close our eyes on some concerns once we've decided in our mind that we like a person (usually in the first few seconds of meeting them). However, this is where you have to detach emotionally, and let your business persona take over.

You have to evaluate all the information received, and decide based on hard facts alone if the hire is right.

Another important piece of advice is to take your time to hire. Often, we rush to fill a much-needed position with someone who is "almost a fit"; however, these types of hires could turn costly in the long term. You might be spending extra time teaching them the necessary skills, or simply regretting your decision later when the candidate doesn't add much value.

Take your time to hire the right person for the job; it allows both parties to think through everything carefully and pass the test of time. It also tests the candidate's level of interest in the job. If the person keeps following up and demonstrates that he or she is still interested in working with you, it's a sign they genuinely care. Finding someone who really wants the job and is committed to you should be one of the top requirements on your list.

Whether it's a consultant you are hiring for a small project, or a manager you are letting manage your career, be careful of who you surround yourself with. Learn from every mistake, and take note for any future hires. Eventually, you will have your list of must-have qualities, which will make your job as the Human Resources Manager of your empire easier.

50

LEARN TO LEAD

Our journey together is coming to a close, and the last and most important piece of advice I can give you is to develop your leadership skills. Not many of us are natural-born leaders. I know I wasn't. It took years of experience, self-affirmations, and acquiring emotional intelligence skills to become a successful leader.

Leadership is a non-negotiable quality for every entrepreneur – and certainly for an online influencer who is shaping people's opinions on a daily basis and trying to grow an online business. It is part of your job to inspire your followers and your employees.

As a manager, you carry the responsibility for people's careers and daily accomplishments. It is a big pressure that pushes you forward. Providing them with the confidence and reassurance they need is what makes a great leader.

As a self-made entrepreneur, you might become a role model for others. In this capacity, you might be giving advice to aspiring influencers and sharing your path.

How do you learn to lead? Each person has different ways of learning, whether it's hiring a professional, attending a workshop, or reading books. For an introvert like myself, it was a combination of multiple learning techniques, including attending a public speaking course at New York University, hiring an acting coach to work on my stage presence, reading countless books on emotional intelligence, practicing my social skills at various events, and most importantly, a constant desire to get better as a leader.

If you are serious about your business scaling big, you must work to develop the qualities that make a great leader.

After all, influence is leadership.

ACKNOWLEDGEMENTS

As I finish this book, my baby boy is peacefully sleeping in his crib. I started writing it early in my pregnancy, so you could say that he's been with me through the book's entire journey. At his young age, only three months, he already knows to perk up every time I point a cellphone camera at him so that he can give me his most irresistible look. He is also making sounds while communicating with his grandparents via Skype as if he can see them.

This makes me think this Gen Alpha baby was born with built-in selfie capabilities and communication skills that my generation could only dream about. I'm equally excited and anxious to see how he'll grow to use technology and, most importantly, how eventually he will be using his own influence. I hope one day he can read this book and be proud of his mom, and that my message will still be relevant. In the meantime, I want to thank him for being such a good sleeper at his young age, which allowed me to turn every moment of his long naps into writing sessions.

All of this wouldn't be possible if I didn't have the most supportive husband, who cheers me up throughout my entrepreneurial journey, even when I decide to write a book in the middle of my first pregnancy while also running and scaling my business.

Special thanks to my team who continues to build on Style Coalition's legacy. Lastly, all the talented influencers we've ever worked with – thank you for inspiring this book and teaching these important lessons. This incredible industry stands tall on the foundation of your passion.

ABOUT THE AUTHOR

Named one of the Top Women in Media by Folio: magazine, Yuli Ziv is an influencer marketing pioneer, and an immigrant entrepreneur who bootstrapped her business from zero to millions. She is the CEO of Style Coalition, a premier influencer marketing platform she founded in 2008, and she has since authored three books on advising success within the fashion, technology and marketing industries; becoming an Amazon best-seller.

As one of the pioneers of social media in the fashion space, in 2007 Yuli launched the user-generated magazine My It Things (sold in 2013). Prior to founding her own ventures, she developed interactive online strategies, under her role as a Creative Director at the leading digital agency, 360i.

Her two books, Fashion 2.0: Blogging Your Way to the Front Row (2011) and Fashion 2.0: Season of Change (2013) were awarded multiple accolades in both the fashion and technology fields.

An internationally known thought-leader, Yuli has delivered speeches at WWD Magic, DLD, Luxury Retail Summit, NY Internet Week, Yale University,

New York University and Fashion Institute of Technology. She has been featured in The New York Times, Financial Times, New York Observer, Wall Street Journal and Forbes.

After earning a BA in Design of Visual Communications from Tel-Aviv University, Yuli continued her studies after immigrating to the United States where she then earned a MFA in Computer Art from the School of Visual Arts New York. Yuli currently lives and works in New York City.